**Everyman's Poetry**

*Everyman, I will go with thee,
and be thy guide*

# Robert Browning

Selected and edited by COLIN GRAHAM

University of Huddersfield

EVERYMAN

J. M. Dent · London

This edition first published by Everyman Paperbacks in 1997
Selection, introduction and other critical material
© J. M. Dent 1997

J. M. Dent
Orion Publishing Group
Orion House
5 Upper St Martin's Lane
London WC2H 9EA

Typeset by Deltatype Ltd, Birkenhead, Merseyside
Printed in Great Britain by
The Guernsey Press Co. Ltd., Guernsey, C.I.

British Library Cataloguing-in-Publication Data
is available upon request.

ISBN 0 460 87893 X

# Contents

# Note on the Author and Editor

ROBERT BROWNING was born on 7 May 1812 in Camberwell, London, and was educated at home, at school in Peckham and briefly at London University. A voracious and eclectic reader from an early age, he wrote his first volume of poetry, *Incondita*, at the age of fourteen, though he subsequently destroyed the manuscript. His first published volume was *Pauline* which appeared anonymously in 1833, sold no copies and was largely ignored by critics. His next volume, *Paracelsus* (1835), was more successful, but failures in play-writing and the perceived obscurity of *Sordello* (1840) meant that his initial fame was short-lived. Between 1841 and 1846 Browning published a series of poems and plays, *Bells and Pomegranates*, which include some of his best-known works such as 'Home-Thoughts, from Abroad', 'The Pied Piper of Hamelin' and 'My Last Duchess'.

In 1845 Browning wrote the first of many letters to Elizabeth Barrett. In the same year, and against the wishes of Elizabeth's father, they began their clandestine courtship. They married secretly and eloped to Italy in 1846. During their married life, spent mainly in Florence, the Brownings' son, Robert Wiedemann Barrett Browning ('Pen') was born and Browning continued to publish collections of poetry, including *Men and Women* in 1855.

After Elizabeth's death in 1861, Browning returned to London. The publication of *Dramatis Personae* (1864) and *The Ring and the Book* (1868–9) confirmed Browning as one of the most eminent of Victorian literary figures. In 1881 the Browning Society was formed to undertake the study of his complex poetry. He continued to write and publish prolifically until his death in Venice on 12 December 1889, the day of publication of his last volume of verse, *Asolando*. He was buried on 31 December 1889 in Poets' Corner, Westminster Abbey.

COLIN GRAHAM is lecturer in English Literature at the University of Huddersfield. He has previously edited Robert Browning, *Men and Women and Other Poems* and Elizabeth Barrett Browning, *Selected*

*Poems*. Forthcoming books include *Ireland and Cultural Theory* (co-edited) and *Introduction to Irish Studies*.

# Chronology of Browning's Life

| Year | Life |
|------|------|
| 1812 | Browning born 7 May at Camberwell, south-east London |
| 1814 | Browning's sister, Sarianna, born |
| c. 1820 | Attends school in Peckham |
| 1826 | Leaves school and is educated at home for two years. Manuscript of a volume of poems (*Incondita*) is completed |
| 1828 | Attends London University |
| 1829 | Leaves London University |
| 1832 | Sees Edmund Kean in *Richard III* |
| 1833 | *Pauline*, his first volume of poetry, published anonymously |
| 1834 | Travels to St Petersburg |
| 1835 | *Paracelsus* published to critical acclaim |
| 1836 | 'Porphyria's Lover' and 'Johannes Agricola' published in *Monthly Repository*. Meets Wordsworth |
| 1837 | *Strafford*, his first play, published and performed at Covent Garden |
| 1838 | First trip to Italy |
| 1840 | *Sordello* published |

# Chronology of his Times

| Year | Literary Context | Historical Events |
|---|---|---|
| 1812 | Dickens born | Napoleon enters Russia, America declares war on Britain |
| 1813 | Jane Austen, *Pride and Prejudice* | East India Company monopoly abolished |
| 1814 | Wordsworth, *The Excursion* | |
| 1820 | Shelley, *Prometheus Unbound* | Accession of George IV |
| 1821 | Death of Keats | |
| 1822 | Matthew Arnold born<br>Death of Shelley | Famine in Ireland |
| 1824 | Death of Byron | |
| 1825 | | Trades unions legalised |
| 1827 | Clare, *Shepherd's Calendar* | |
| 1829 | | Catholic emancipation |
| 1830 | Tennyson, *Poems, Chiefly Lyrical* | Accession of William IV |
| 1832 | Death of Walter Scott | First Reform Act |
| 1833 | Carlyle, *Sartor Resartus* | Abolition of slavery in British Empire |
| 1834 | Death of Coleridge | Trials of Tolpuddle Martyrs |
| 1837 | Dickens, *Oliver Twist* | Accession of Victoria |
| 1838 | Dickens, *Nicholas Nickleby* | Anti-Corn Law League established |
| 1840 | Dickens, *Old Curiosity Shop* | |

| Year | Life |
|------|------|
| 1841 | *Pippa Passes* published, the first of a series of works under the collective title *Bells and Pomegranates* |
| 1842 | *King Victor and King Charles; Dramatic Lyrics* |
| 1843 | *Bells and Pomegranates IV* and *V* |
| 1844 | Visits Italy and publishes *Colombe's Birthday* |
| 1845 | Writes first of many letters to Elizabeth Barrett, and begins clandestine courtship. *Dramatic Lyrics and Romances* published as *Bells and Pomegranates VII* |
| 1846 | *Luria* and *A Soul's Tragedy* (plays) published, making up final number of *Bells and Pomegranates*. Secretly marries Elizabeth Barrett. They elope to Italy |
| 1847 | The Brownings move from Pisa to their house, Casa Guidi, in Florence |
| 1849 | *Poems* (2 volumes) published, collecting and (partly) revising all Browning's previously published poetry with the exception of *Sordello*. Browning's son, Robert Wiedemann Barrett Browning ('Pen') is born. Browning's mother dies |
| 1850 | *Christmas-Eve and Easter-Day* published |
| 1851 | Travels to Paris and then to London for first time since elopement |
| 1852 | 'Essay on Shelley' published |
| 1853–4 | Resident in Italy, with other expatriate acquaintances |
| 1855 | *Men and Women and Other Poems* published without critical success |
| 1856 | Substantial legacies left to Browning and Elizabeth by John Kenyon |

| Year | Literary Context | Historical Events |
|------|------------------|-------------------|
| 1841 | Carlyle, *On Heroes and Hero-Worship* | Robert Peel becomes Prime Minister |
| 1842 | Tennyson, *Poems* | |
| 1843 | Death of Southey Wordsworth becomes Poet Laureate | |
| 1844 | Elizabeth Barrett Browning, *Poems* | |
| 1846 | | Corn Law abolished |
| 1847 | Charlotte Brontë, *Jane Eyre* Emily Brontë, *Wuthering Heights* | |
| 1848 | Thackeray, *Vanity Fair* | Revolutions in Europe |
| 1849 | Ruskin, *Seven Lamps of Architecture* | |
| 1850 | Death of Wordsworth Tennyson, *In Memoriam* Tennyson made Laureate | |
| 1851 | Ruskin, *Stones of Venice* | Great Exhibition |
| 1852 | Thackeray, *Henry Esmond* | Fall of French Republic |
| 1853 | Matthew Arnold, *Poems* | |
| 1854 | Dickens, *Hard Times* | Crimean War begins |
| 1855 | Matthew Arnold, *Poems, Second Series* | Palmerston becomes Prime Minister |
| 1856 | Thomas Hughes, *Tom Brown's Schooldays* | Treaty of Paris |

| Year | Life |
| --- | --- |
| 1857 | Elizabeth's father dies |
| 1859 | The Brownings take in Walter Savage Landor who has quarrelled with his family |
| 1860 | Browning buys the 'Old Yellow Book' from a market stall in Florence, containing the documents which will form the basis of *The Ring and the Book* |
| 1861 | Elizabeth Barrett Browning dies. Browning leaves Italy with Pen |
| 1862 | Settles in London |
| 1863 | *The Poetical Works* (3 volumes) published (including *Sordello*) |
| 1864 | *Dramatis Personae* published, marking the beginning of the heights of Browning's critical reputation |
| 1866 | Browning's father dies |
| 1867 | Receives honorary MA from Oxford University |
| 1868 | *The Poetical Works* (6 volumes) |
| 1868–9 | *The Ring and the Book* published in four monthly parts |
| 1869 | Presented to Queen Victoria |
| 1871 | *Balaustion's Adventures* and *Prince Hohenstiel-Schwangau* |
| 1872 | *Fifine at the Fair* |
| 1873 | *Red Cotton Night-Cap Country* |
| 1875 | *Aristophanes' Apology* and *The Inn Album* |

| Year | Literary Context | Historical Events |
|---|---|---|
| 1857 | Trollope, *Barchester Towers* | Indian Mutiny |
| | Elizabeth Barrett Browning, *Aurora Leigh* | |
| 1858 | George Eliot, *Scenes of Clerical Life* | British Crown assumes control of India |
| 1859 | Darwin, *Origin of Species* | Construction of Suez Canal begins |
| 1860 | George Eliot, *Mill on the Floss* | |
| 1861 | J. S. Mill, *Utilitarianism* | Prince Albert dies. Beginning of American Civil War |
| 1862 | Christina Rossetti, *Goblin Market and Other Poems* | |
| 1863 | Death of Thackeray | |
| 1864 | Trollope, *Can You Forgive Her?* | |
| 1865 | Yeats born | American Civil War ends |
| | Kipling born | |
| 1866 | Swinburne, *Poems and Ballads* | Last cholera epidemic in Britain |
| 1867 | Water Bagehot, *English Constitution* | Second Reform Act |
| 1868 | William Morris, *Earthly Paradise* | Gladstone becomes Prime Minister |
| 1869 | Matthew Arnold, *Culture and Anarchy* | |
| 1870 | Death of Dickens | Franco-Prussian War |
| 1871 | Darwin, *Descent of Man* | Paris commune |
| 1872 | Tennyson, *Gareth and Lynette* | |
| 1873 | Death of J. S. Mill | Gladstone government resigns |
| 1874 | Hardy, *Far From the Madding Crowd* | Gold Coast annexed |

| Year | Life |
| --- | --- |
| 1876 | *Pacchiarotto and How He Worked in Distemper: with Other Poems* |
| 1877 | *The Agamemnon of Aeschylus* |
| 1878 | *La Saisiaz* and *The Two Poets of Croisic*. Browning visits Italy for the first time since Elizabeth's death |
| 1879 | *Dramatic Idyls* |
| 1880 | *Dramatic Idyls: Second Series* |
| 1881 | The Browning Society founded |
| 1883 | *Jocoseria* |
| 1884 | *Feristah's Fancies* |
| 1887 | *Parleyings with Certain People of Importance in Their Day* |
| 1888–9 | *The Poetical Works* (16 volumes) |
| 1889 | *Asolando* published on 12 December. Browning dies the same day in Venice. Buried in Poets' Corner, Westminster Abbey on 31 December |

| Year | Literary Context | Historical Events |
|------|------------------|-------------------|
| 1876 | Twain, *The Adventures of Tom Sawyer* | Victoria proclaimed Empress of India |
| 1877 | Henry James, *The American* | |
| 1878 | Gilbert and Sullivan, *HMS Pinafore* | Congress of Berlin |
| 1879 | George Meredith, *The Egoist* | Zulu War |
| 1880 | Death of George Eliot | Gladstone's second government |
| 1881 | Henry James, *Portrait of a Lady* | Death of Disraeli |
| 1882 | Virginia Woolf born<br>James Joyce born | British occupation of Egypt |
| 1885 | Ezra Pound born | Gordon dies at Khartoum |
| 1886 | Hardy, *The Mayor of Casterbridge* | Failure of First Home Rule Bill |
| 1887 | Hardy, *The Woodlanders* | Victoria's Golden Jubilee |
| 1888 | William Morris, *A Dream of John Ball* | |
| 1889 | Death of Wilkie Collins | London Dock strike |

# Introduction

According to George Eliot, 'in Browning's best poems he makes us feel that what we took for obscurity in him was superficiality in ourselves.'[1] As Eliot suggests, Browning's poems often rely for their profundity, complexity and humour on the interplay between the obscure and the apparently 'superficial'. While this is part of their joy, it is also vital to their seriousness and their impact. Browning's poetry is always ready to examine its own language and assumptions with intellectual vigour and in doing this it often prefers to use what appears to be the ephemeral, the colloquial, along with what is ultimately the unnerving and disturbing.

Browning is best known for his dramatic monologues and for 'The Pied Piper of Hamelin', one of those 'children's' writings which becomes repeated, often out of context and without acknowledgement, in more popular cultural forms. The dramatic monologues, poems such as 'My Last Duchess', 'Porphyria's Lover' and 'Soliloquy of the Spanish Cloister', represent Browning's most unique achievement in terms of poetic form. Their expression of 'personae', the inner minds of the characters who 'speak' the poems, are powerful enough simply on the level of character and dramatisation, which he manages with as much skill as any poet. But the dramatic monologues are always more than the evocation of the 'character' of one individual. They become examinations of the psychological processes of self-delusion, self-justification and blank conviction in which the language used becomes integral to the fragile nature of the speaker's psyche.

In 'Porphyria's Lover' the horror of the murder is hidden by the speaker in the trappings of a standardised poetic atmosphere and a near-logical turn of argument. The poem begins with lovers sheltering from the elements, and the binary contrast of the 'cottage warm'. This gentle, comforting beginning is disrupted when the lover looks at Porphyria, realises she loves him, and 'debates' what to do; here, with this rather legalistic turn of phrase, the poem most obviously switches register, the fairy tale intertwining with the Gothic in the same way that the lover winds

Porphyria's hair 'Three times her little throat around'. Crucial to reading the dramatic monologues is the recognition that Browning's ways of undermining the argument of his speakers are integral to the speaker's voices. Rather than insisting on passing a judgement, Browning refuses to remove himself to a position where he would become moral arbiter of these characters. Hence the devastating weight of the lover's lines, 'No pain felt she;/ I am quite sure she felt no pain'. With Browning the poet withdrawn, the reaffirmation here, and the pause forced by the punctuation and the end of the line, capture that moment of doubt, when the terror of the murder registers with the lover and is quickly dismissed. And from here there is only one way for the poem to go, back into its fairy tale, which has now become inverted; so he sits looking at her 'smiling little rosy head' (an image of appropriate, horrific disembodiment). Having got this far, where there is an almost seamless argument with one moment of doubt passed over, Browning does not stop. Rather he goes on to make full use of his reluctance simply to condemn; the twisted nature of the poem unravels in a piece of indisputable logic: 'all night long we have not stirred,/ And yet God has not said a word'. For Browning's contemporaries God's echoing silence would have touched the rawest of nerves; if the poem could be dismissed, up until this point, as the ravings of a madman (as the original title 'Madhouse Cells I' might have suggested), the dénouement makes it clear that such a dismissal and distancing would be too easy and, ironically, self-delusory.

Browning's other soliloquists show similar characteristics to Porphyria's lover, but increasingly the form is used for unwitting self-revelation as well as psycho-study. The speaker of 'My Last Duchess' can easily be decoded as another murderer – the mystery of this poem hinges as much on what the envoy spoken to manages to unravel from the Duke's story. Will he advise that his master allow his daughter to marry this man? How could he? What evidence is there? In 'Soliloquy of the Spanish Cloister' the 'spoken' nature of the dramatic monologue is given its fullest expression. What other poet could begin a poem with 'Gr-r-r – '? The monk's irritation, his institutionalised, irrational hatred of Brother Lawrence is on a microcosmic scale the 'irrationality' of the Duke's displeasure and paranoia in 'My Last Duchess' and the lover's loss of rationality in 'Porphyria's Lover'. Browning's monk spits and froths wonderfully and his 'Hy, Zy, Hine' makes humorously the same point made in other dramatic monologues, Language is the key, here inadequately expressing the monk's loathing, becoming confused in his Latin, ending in pathetic insult, whereas in other poems language rolls along with the argument of the speakers, but out of control of the logic of the 'rational'.

The tropes of language, control and disorder are continuous themes in Browning. In 'The Pied Piper of Hamelin' he typically makes use of his ability to particularise a narrative through anecdote, eccentricity and linguistic sleight, and the result is a story which, like the monologues, has a cohesion and a 'sense' of its own which is disturbingly parallel to 'normality'. The chaos of Hamelin infested by rats is made civic and political as well as metaphoric, while the Piper becomes one in a long line of Browning's characters who exhibits an eccentric and dark control through a skill or art (Fra Lippo Lippi and Andrea del Sarto are other obvious, different examples). In this sense the Piper parallels Browning the poet in creating a darkness out of apparent security. The Mayor and Corporation are shocked out of their complacency when they refuse to pay their proper dues just as a reader of Browning, wishing for 'My Last Duchess' to be a mournful love poem, or for 'Porphyria's Lover' to be a heroic poem of tragic love, will find themselves shaken awake by the untouchable personalities of Browning's speakers. 'The Pied Piper', typically of Browning, brings together what might be a dreamy fairy tale with his fascination with death, destruction and forces outside the understanding or control of the individual or society ('Childe Roland to the Dark Tower Came' functions in a similar way).

If these seem like weighty claims to make for any poet, it is probably comforting for a contemporary reader to know that the richness, and at times the difficulty, of Browning was the main feature registered during his lifetime by critics of his poetry (both those who derided and those who praised him). George Eliot's comments, quoted at the beginning of this Introduction (p. xvi), were largely a reaction to what had even by then become typical criticism of Browning as an obscure poet. *Sordello* (1840) received treatment from the reviewer in the *Athenaeum* which was more open than most, but nevertheless caught the sentiment of those bemused and frustrated by Browning:

It is really time that this sort of thing should, if possible, be stopped. Here is another book of madness and mysticism – another

melancholy specimen of power wantonly wasted, and talent deliber-
ately perverted . . . Why should a man who, with so little apparent
labour, can write naturally and well, take so much apparent labour
to write affectedly and ill? . . . [We] are inclined to clear his honesty at
the expense of his powers, and to conclude that he is obscure, not so
much because he has the vanity to be thought original, as because he
lacks sufficient genius to make himself clear.[2]

William Morris, like George Eliot, was one who came to Browning's
defence on the charge of obscurity when reviewing *Men and Women*
for the *Oxford and Cambridge Magazine.* Browning's obscurity, he
claimed, was 'one of the very grandest of all God's gifts to men [and]
we must not think it hard if we have sometimes to exercise thought
over a great poem'.

However convincingly Eliot and Morris argue for Browning's
poetry against the charges of obscurity, they are both careful to
draw a distinction between this and what is 'difficult', and
Browning's poetry is certainly difficult. Its tone is unique for its
time, weaving the colloquial with the intellectual in a way which
undermines some of the implicit hierarchies of language. Added to
this is the slippery nature of the poetic persona, always lurking
behind the dramatic persona, but never staying still long enough to
be given a moral shape. In Browning's poetry what often looks like
obscurity is the sense of insecurity the reader feels on being deserted
by the personality of the poet (which is expected to be the mainstay
of the poem). In his mimicry, intellectualism and questioning of
romantic notions of the sanctity of poetic self-expression Browning
prefigures (and at times outdoes) the modernists who so often
admired him. In using visual art as a predominant metaphor for the
process of writing poetry, Browning sought to find a new concep-
tion of how the life of the poet could be tranformed into his or her
creations. Like Lippo Lippi or del Sarto, Browning is in everything
he makes (like them, often bizarrely and unexpectedly so); but as
with Browning's poetry, their art is not continual self-portraiture –
they paint myth, legend, religion and history, and the barriers
between them and their subjects dissipate and merge. If those
barriers remain for the reader of Browning, then he remains
obscure; if they are challenged and fade, then Browning becomes
energetic, complex and playful, a writer of astonishing depth and
often deadly humour.

                                                    COLIN GRAHAM

# Robert Browning

# My Last Duchess

## Ferrara

That's my last Duchess painted on the wall,
Looking as if she were alive. I call
That piece a wonder, now: Frà Pandolf's hands
Worked busily a day, and there she stands.
Will't please you sit and look at her? I said
'Frà Pandolf' by design, for never read
Strangers like you that pictured countenance,
The depth and passion of its earnest glance,
But to myself they turned (since none puts by
The curtain I have drawn for you, but I)                      10
And seemed as they would ask me, if they durst,
How such a glance came there; so, not the first
Are you to turn and ask thus. Sir, 't was not
Her husband's presence only, called that spot
Of joy into the Duchess' cheek: perhaps
Frà Pandolf chanced to say 'Her mantle laps
Over my lady's wrist too much,' or 'Paint
Must never hope to reproduce the faint
Half-flush that dies along her throat:' such stuff
Was courtesy, she thought, and cause enough          20
For calling up that spot of joy. She had
A heart . . . how shall I say? . . . too soon made glad,
Too easily impressed; she liked whate'er
She looked on, and her looks went everywhere.
Sir, 't was all one! My favour at her breast,
The dropping of the daylight in the West,
The bough of cherries some officious fool
Broke in the orchard for her, the white mule
She rode with round the terrace – all and each
Would draw from her alike the approving speech,          30
Or blush, at least. She thanked men, – good! but thanked
Somehow . . . I know not how . . . as if she ranked
My gift of a nine-hundred-years-old name

With anybody's gift. Who'd stoop to blame
This sort of trifling? Even had you skill
In speech – (which I have not) – to make your will
Quite clear to such an one, and say, 'Just this
Or that in you disgusts me; here you miss,
Or there exceed the mark' – and if she let
Herself be lessoned so, nor plainly set                              40
Her wits to yours, forsooth, and made excuse,
– E'en then would be some stooping; and I choose
Never to stoop. Oh sir, she smiled, no doubt,
Whene'er I passed her, but who passed without
Much the same smile? This grew; I gave commands;
Then all smiles stopped together. There she stands
As if alive. Will't please you rise? We'll meet
The company below, then. I repeat,
The Count your master's known munificence
Is ample warrant that no just pretence                              50
Of mine for dowry will be disallowed;
Though his fair daughter's self, as I avowed
At starting, is my object. Nay, we'll go
Together down, sir. Notice Neptune, though,
Taming a sea-horse, thought a rarity,
Which Claus of Innsbruck cast in bronze for me!

# Soliloquy of the Spanish Cloister

### 1

Gr-r-r – there go, my heart's abhorrence!
    Water your damned flower-pots, do!
If hate killed men, Brother Lawrence,
    God's blood, would not mine kill you!
What? your myrtle-bush wants trimming?
    Oh, that rose has prior claims –
Needs its leaden vase filled brimming?
    Hell dry you up with its flames!

### 2

At the meal we sit together:
    Salve tibi! I must hear
Wise talk of the kind of weather,
    Sort of season, time of year:
Not a plenteous cork-crop: scarcely
    Dare we hope oak-galls, I doubt:
What's the Latin name for 'parsley'?
    What's the Greek name for Swine's Snout?

### 3

Whew! We'll have our platter burnished,
    Laid with care on our own shelf!
With a fire-new spoon we're furnished,
    And a goblet for ourself,
Rinsed like something sacrificial
    Ere't is fit to touch our chaps –
Marked with L. for our initial!
    (He-he! There his lily snaps!)

### 4

Saint, forsooth! While brown Dolores
Squats outside the Convent bank
With Sanchicha, telling stories,
    Steeping tresses in the tank,

Blue-black, lustrous, thick like horsehairs,
  – Can't I see his dead eye glow,           30
Bright as't were a Barbary corsair's?
  (That is, if he'd let it show!)


### 5

When he finishes reflection,
  Knife and fork he never lays
Cross-wise, to my recollection,
  As do I, in Jesu's praise.
I the Trinity illustrate,
  Drinking watered orange-pulp –
In three sips the Arian frustrate;
  While he drains his at one gulp.           40


### 6

Oh, those melons? If he's able
  We're to have a feast! so nice!
One goes to the Abbot's table,
  All of us get each a slice.
How go on your flowers? None double?
  Not one fruit-sort can you spy?
Strange! – And I, too, at such trouble,
  Keep them close-nipped on the sly!


### 7

There's a great text in Galatians,
  Once you trip on it, entails           50
Twenty-nine distinct damnations,
  One sure, if another fails:
If I trip him just a-dying,
  Sure of heaven as sure can be,
Spin him round and send him flying
  Off to hell, a Manichee?


### 8

Or, my scrofulous French novel
  On grey paper with blunt type!
Simply glance at it, you grovel
  Hand and foot in Belial's gripe:           60

If I double down its pages
    At the woeful sixteenth print,
When he gathers his greengages,
    Ope a sieve and slip it in't?

9

Or, there's Satan! – one might venture
    Pledge one's soul to him, yet leave
Such a flaw in the indenture
    As he'd miss till, past retrieve,
Blasted lay that rose-acacia
    We're so proud of! Hy, Zy, Hine . . .                    70
'St, there's Vespers! Plena gratiâ
    Ave, Virgo! Gr-r-r – you swine!

# Johannes Agricola in Meditation

There's heaven above, and night by night
   I look right through its gorgeous roof;
No suns and moons though e'er so bright
   Avail to stop me; splendour-proof
I keep the broods of stars aloof:
For I intend to get to God,
   For 't is to God I speed so fast,
For in God's breast, my own abode,
   Those shoals of dazzling glory, passed,
I lay my spirit down at last.                                    10
I lie where I have always lain,
   God smiles as he has always smiled;
Ere suns and moons could wax and wane,
   Ere stars were thundergirt, or piled
The heavens, God thought on me his child;
Ordained a life for me, arrayed
   Its circumstances every one
To the minutest; ay, God said
   This head this hand should rest upon
Thus, ere he fashioned star or sun.                              20
And having thus created me,
   Thus rooted me, he bade me grow,
Guiltless for ever, like a tree
   That buds and blooms, nor seeks to know
   The law by which it prospers so:
But sure that thought and word and deed
   All go to swell his love for me,
Me, made because that love had need
   Of something irreversibly
Pledged solely its content to be.                                30
Yes, yes, a tree which must ascend,
   No poison-gourd foredoomed to stoop.
I have God's warrant, could I blend
   All hideous sins, as in a cup,
To drink the mingled venoms up;

Secure my nature will convert
    The draught to blossoming gladness fast:
While sweet dews turn to the gourd's hurt,
    And bloat, and while they bloat it, blast,
As from the first its lot was cast.         40
For as I lie, smiled on, full-fed
    By unexhausted power to bless,
I gaze below on hell's fierce bed,
    And those its waves of flame oppress,
Swarming in ghastly wretchedness;
Whose life on earth aspired to be
    One altar-smoke, so pure! – to win
If not love like God's love for me,
    At least to keep his anger in;
And all their striving turned to sin!        50
    Priest, doctor, hermit, monk grown white
With prayer, the broken-hearted nun,
    The martyr, the wan acolyte,
The incense-swinging child, – undone
Before God fashioned star or sun!
God, whom I praise; how could I praise,
    If such as I might understand,
Make out, and reckon on, his ways,
    And bargain for his love, and stand,
Paying a price, at his right hand?        60

# Porphyria's Lover

The rain set early in to-night,
   The sullen wind was soon awake,
It tore the elm-tops down for spite,
   And did its worst to vex the lake:
I listened with heart fit to break.
When glided in Porphyria; straight
   She shut the cold out and the storm,
And kneeled and made the cheerless grate
   Blaze up, and all the cottage warm;
Which done, she rose, and from her form      10
Withdrew the dripping cloak and shawl,
   And laid her soiled gloves by, untied
Her hat and let the damp hair fall,
   And, last, she sat down by my side
And called me. When no voice replied,
She put my arm about her waist,
   And made her smooth white shoulder bare,
And all her yellow hair displaced,
   And, stooping, made my cheek lie there,
And spread, o'er all, her yellow hair,      20
Murmuring how she loved me – she
   Too weak, for all her heart's endeavour,
To set its struggling passion free
   From pride, and vainer ties dissever,
And give herself to me for ever.
But passion sometimes would prevail,
   Nor could to-night's gay feast restrain
A sudden thought of one so pale
   For love of her, and all in vain:
So, she was come through wind and rain.      30
Be sure I looked up at her eyes
   Proud, very proud; at last I knew
Porphyria worshipped me; surprise
   Made my heart swell, and still it grew
While I debated what to do.

That moment she was mine, mine, fair,
　　Perfectly pure and good: I found
A thing to do, and all her hair
　　In one long yellow string I wound
Three times her little throat around,　　　　　40
And strangled her. No pain felt she;
　　I am quite sure she felt no pain.
As a shut bud that holds a bee,
　　I warily oped her lids: again
Laughed the blue eyes without a stain.
And I untightened next the tress
　　About her neck; her cheek once more
Blushed bright beneath my burning kiss:
　　I propped her head up as before,
Only, this time *my* shoulder bore　　　　　50
Her head, which droops upon it still:
　　The smiling rosy little head,
So glad it has its utmost will,
　　That all it scorned at once is fled,
And I, its love, am gained instead!
Porphyria's love: she guessed not how
　　Her darling one wish would be heard.
And thus we sit together now,
　　And all night long we have not stirred,
And yet God has not said a word!　　　　　60

# The Pied Piper of Hamelin

## A Child's Story

(written for, and inscribed to, W. M. The Younger)

### 1

Hamelin Town's in Brunswick,
  By famous Hanover city;
The river Weser, deep and wide,
Washes its wall on the southern side;
A pleasanter spot you never spied;
  But, when begins my ditty,
Almost five hundred years ago,
To see the townsfolk suffer so
  From vermin, was a pity.

### 2

  Rats!                                                              10
They fought the dogs and killed the cats,
  And bit the babies in the cradles,
And ate the cheeses out of the vats,
  And licked the soup from the cooks' own ladles,
Split open the kegs of salted sprats,
Made nests inside men's Sunday hats,
And even spoiled the women's chats
  By drowning their speaking
  With shrieking and squeaking
In fifty different sharps and flats.                                20

### 3

At last the people in a body
  To the Town Hall came flocking:
''T is clear,' cried they, 'our Mayor's a noddy;
  And as for our Corporation – shocking
To think we buy gowns lined with ermine

For dolts that can't or won't determine
What's best to rid us of our vermin!
You hope, because you're old and obese,
To find in the furry civic robe ease?
Rouse up, sirs! Give your brains a racking                    30
To find the remedy we're lacking,
Or, sure as fate, we'll send you packing!'
At this the Mayor and Corporation
Quaked with a mighty consternation

4

An hour they sat in council,
    At length the Mayor broke silence:
'For a guilder I'd my ermine gown sell,
    I wish I were a mile hence!
It's easy to bid one rack one's brain –
I'm sure my poor head aches again,                    40
I've scratched it so, and all in vain.
Oh for a trap, a trap, a trap!'
Just as he said this, what should hap
At the chamber door but a gentle tap?
'Bless us,' cried the Mayor, 'what's that?'
(With the Corporation as he sat,
Looking little though wondrous fat;
Nor brighter was his eye, nor moister
Than a too-long-opened oyster,
Save when at noon his paunch grew mutinous                    50
For a plate of turtle green and glutinous)
'Only a scraping of shoes on the mat?
Anything like the sound of a rat
Makes my heart go pit-a-pat!'

5

'Come in!' – the Mayor cried, looking bigger
And in did come the strangest figure!
His queer long coat from heel to head
Was half of yellow and half of red,
And he himself was tall and thin,
With sharp blue eyes, each like a pin,                    60

And light loose hair, yet swarthy skin
No tuft on cheek nor beard on chin,
But lips where smiles went out and in;
There was no guessing his kith and kin:
And nobody could enough admire
The tall man and his quaint attire.
Quoth one: 'It's as my great-grandsire,
Starting up at the Trump of Doom's tone,
Had walked this way from his painted tombstone!'

6

He advanced to the council-table:       70
And, 'Please your honours,' said he, 'I'm able,
By means of a secret charm, to draw
   All creatures living beneath the sun,
   That creep or swim or fly or run,
After me so as you never saw!
And I chiefly use my charm
On creatures that do people harm,
The mole and toad and newt and viper;
And people call me the Pied Piper.'
(And here they noticed round his neck       80
   A scarf of red and yellow stripe,
To match with his coat of the self-same cheque;
   And at the scarf's end hung a pipe;
And his fingers, they noticed, were ever straying
As if impatient to be playing
Upon this pipe, as low it dangled
Over his vesture so old-fangled.)
'Yet,' said he, 'poor piper as I am,
In Tartary I freed the Cham,
   Last June, from his huge swarms of gnats;       90
I eased in Asia the Nizam
   Of a monstrous brood of vampyre-bats:
And as for what your brain bewilders,
   If I can rid your town of rats
Will you give me a thousand guilders?'
'One? fifty thousand!' – was the exclamation
Of the astonished Mayor and Corporation.

### 7

Into the street the Piper stept,
  Smiling first a little smile,
As if he knew what magic slept
  In his quiet pipe the while;                    100
Then, like a musical adept,
To blow the pipe his lips he wrinkled,
And green and blue his sharp eyes twinkled,
Like a candle-flame where salt is sprinkled;
And ere three shrill notes the pipe uttered,
You heard as if an army muttered;
And the muttering grew to a grumbling;
And the grumbling grew to a mighty rumbling;
And out of the houses the rats came tumbling.     110
Great rats, small rats, lean rats, brawny rats,
Brown rats, black rats, grey rats, tawny rats,
Grave old plodders, gay young friskers,
  Fathers, mothers, uncles, cousins,
Cocking tails and pricking whiskers,
  Families by tens and dozens,
Brothers, sisters, husbands, wives —
Followed the Piper for their lives.
From street to street he piped advancing,
And step for step they followed dancing,          120
Until they came to the river Weser,
  Wherein all plunged and perished!
– Save one who, stout as Julius Cæsar,
Swam across and lived to carry
  (As he, the manuscript he cherished)
To Rat-land home his commentary:
Which was, 'At the first shrill notes of the pipe,
I heard a sound as of scraping tripe,
And putting apples, wondrous ripe,
Into a cider-press's gripe:                        130
And a moving away of pickle-tub-boards,
And a leaving ajar of conserve-cupboards,
And a drawing the corks of train-oil-flasks,
And a breaking the hoops of butter-casks:
And it seemed as if a voice
  (Sweeter far than bý harp or bý psaltery

Is breathed) called out, "Oh rats, rejoice!
    The world is grown to one vast drysaltery!
So munch on, crunch on, take your nuncheon,
Breakfast, supper, dinner, luncheon!"                    140
And just as a bulky sugar-puncheon,
All ready staved, like a great sun shone
Glorious scarce an inch before me,
Just as methought it said, "Come, bore me!"
– I found the Weser rolling o'er me.'


                            8
You should have heard the Hamelin people
Ringing the bells till they rocked the steeple.
'Go,' cried the Mayor, 'and get long poles,
Poke out the nests and block up the holes!
Consult with carpenters and builders,                    150
And leave in our town not even a trace
Of the rats!' – when suddenly, up the face
Of the Piper perked in the market-place,
With a, 'First, if you please, my thousand guilders!'


                            9
A thousand guilders! The Mayor looked blue;
So did the Corporation too.
For council dinners made rare havoc
With Claret, Moselle, Vin-de-Grave, Hock;
And half the money would replenish
Their cellar's biggest butt with Rhenish.                    160
To pay this sum to a wandering fellow
With a gipsy coat of red and yellow!
'Beside,' quoth the Mayor with a knowing wink,
'Our business was done at the river's brink;
We saw with our eyes the vermin sink,
And what's dead can't come to life, I think.
So, friend, we're not the folks to shrink
From the duty of giving you something for drink,
And a matter of money to put in your poke;
But as for the guilders, what we spoke                    170
Of them, as you very well know, was in joke.

Beside, our losses have made us thrifty.
A thousand guilders! Come, take fifty!'

### 10

The Piper's face fell, and he cried
'No trifling! I can't wait, beside!
I've promised to visit by dinnertime
Bagdat, and accept the prime
Of the Head-Cook's pottage, all he's rich in,
For having left, in the Caliph's kitchen,
Of a nest of scorpions no survivor:                        180
With him I proved no bargain-driver,
With you, don't think I'll bate a stiver!
And folks who put me in a passion
May find me pipe after another fashion.'

### 11

'How?' cried the Mayor, 'd'ye think I brook
Being worse treated than a Cook?
Insulted by a lazy ribald
With idle pipe and vesture piebald?
You threaten us, fellow? Do your worst,
Blow your pipe there till you burst!'                      190

### 12

Once more he stept into the street
    And to his lips again
    Laid his long pipe of smooth straight cane;
And ere he blew three notes (such sweet
Soft notes as yet musician's cunning
    Never gave the enraptured air)
There was a rustling that seemed like a bustling
Of merry crowds justling at pitching and hustling,
Small feet were pattering, wooden shoes clattering,
Little hands clapping and little tongues chattering,       200
And, like fowls in a farm-yard when barley is scattering,
Out came the children running.
All the little boys and girls,
With rosy cheeks and flaxen curls,
And sparkling eyes and teeth like pearls,

Tripping and skipping, ran merrily after
The wonderful music with shouting and laughter.

### 13

The Mayor was dumb, and the Council stood
As if they were changed into blocks of wood,
Unable to move a step, or cry                                    210
To the children merrily skipping by,
– Could only follow with the eye
That joyous crowd at the Piper's back.
But how the Mayor was on the rack,
And the wretched Council's bosoms beat,
As the Piper turned from the High Street
To where the Weser rolled its waters
Right in the way of their sons and daughters!
However he turned from South to West,
And to Koppelberg Hill his steps addressed,              220
And after him the children pressed;
Great was the joy in every breast.
'He never can cross that mighty top!
He's forced to let the piping drop,
And we shall see our children stop!'
When, lo, as they reached the mountain-side,
A wondrous portal opened wide,
As if a cavern was suddenly hollowed;
And the Piper advanced and the children followed,
And when all were in to the very last,                        230
The door in the mountain-side shut fast.
Did I say, all? No! One was lame,
    And could not dance the whole of the way;
And in after years, if you would blame
    His sadness, he was used to say, –
'It's dull in our town since my playmates left!
I can't forget that I'm bereft
Of all the pleasant sights they see,
Which the Piper also promised me.
For he led us, he said, to a joyous land,               240
Joining the town and just at hand,
Where waters gushed and fruit-trees grew
And flowers put forth a fairer hue,
And everything was strange and new;

The sparrows were brighter than peacocks here,
And their dogs outran our fallow deer,
And honey-bees had lost their stings,
And horses were born with eagles' wings:
And just as I became assured
My lame foot would be speedily cured,                    250
The music stopped and I stood still,
And found myself outside the hill,
Left alone against my will,
To go now limping as before,
And never hear of that country more!'

### 14

Alas, alas for Hamelin!
  There came into many a burgher's pate
  A text which says that heaven's gate
  Opes to the rich at as easy rate
As the needle's eye takes a camel in!                    260
The mayor sent East, West, North and South,
To offer the Piper, by word of mouth,
  Wherever it was men's lot to find him,
Silver and gold to his heart's content,
If he'd only return the way he went,
  And bring the children behind him.
But when they saw 't was a lost endeavour,
And Piper and dancers were gone for ever,
They made a decree that lawyers never
  Should think their records dated duly               270
If, after the day of the month and year,
These words did not as well appear,
'And so long after what happened here
  On the Twenty-second of July,
Thirteen hundred and seventy-six:'
And the better in memory to fix
The place of the children's last retreat,
They called it, the Pied Piper's Street –
Where any one playing on pipe or tabor
Was sure for the future to lose his labour.              280
Nor suffered they hostelry or tavern
  To shock with mirth a street so solemn;

But opposite the place of the cavern
   They wrote the story on a column,
And on the great church-window painted
The same, to make the world acquainted
How their children were stolen away,
And there it stands to this very day.
And I must not omit to say
That in Transylvania there's a tribe          290
Of alien people who ascribe
The outlandish ways and dress
On which their neighbours lay such stress,
To their fathers and mothers having risen
Out of some subterraneous prison
Into which they were trepanned
Long time ago in a mighty band
Out of Hamelin town in Brunswick land,
But how or why, they don't understand.

15

So, Willy, let me and you be wipers          300
Of scores out with all men – especially pipers!
And, whether they pipe us free fróm rats or fróm mice,
If we've promised them aught, let us keep our promise!

# Home-Thoughts, from Abroad

### 1

Oh, to be in England
Now that April's there,
And whoever wakes in England
Sees, some morning, unaware,
That the lowest boughs and the brushwood sheaf
Round the elm-tree bole are in tiny leaf,
While the chaffinch sings on the orchard bough
In England – now!

### 2

And after April, when May follows,
And the whitethroat builds, and all the swallows!     10
Hark, where my blossomed pear-tree in the hedge
Leans to the field and scatters on the clover
Blossoms and dewdrops – at the bent spray's edge –
That's the wise thrush; he sings each song twice over,
Lest you should think he never could recapture
The first fine careless rapture!
And though the fields look rough with hoary dew
All will be gay when noontide wakes anew
The buttercups, the little children's dower
– Far brighter than this gaudy melon-flower!         20

# Home-Thoughts, from the Sea

Nobly, nobly Cape Saint Vincent to the North-west died away;
Sunset ran, one glorious blood-red, reeking into Cadiz Bay;
Bluish 'mid the burning water, full in face Trafalgar lay;
In the dimmest North-east distance dawned Gibraltar grand
    and gray;
'Here and here did England help me: how can I help England?'
    – say,
Whoso turns as I, this evening, turn to God to praise and pray,
While Jove's planet rises yonder, silent over Africa.

# The Bishop Orders His Tomb at Saint Praxed's Church

[Rome, 15--]

Vanity, saith the preacher, vanity!
Draw round my bed: is Anselm keeping back?
Nephews – sons mine . . . ah God, I know not! Well –
She, men would have to be your mother once,
Old Gandolf envied me, so fair she was!
What's done is done, and she is dead beside,
Dead long ago, and I am Bishop since,
And as she died so must we die ourselves,
And thence ye may perceive the world's a dream.
Life, how and what is it? As here I lie                        10
In this state-chamber, dying by degrees,
Hours and long hours in the dead night, I ask
'Do I live, am I dead?' Peace, peace seems all.
Saint Praxed's ever was the church for peace;
And so, about this tomb of mine. I fought
With tooth and nail to save my niche, ye know:
– Old Gandolf cozened me, despite my care;
Shrewd was that snatch from out the corner South
He graced his carrion with, God curse the same!
Yet still my niche is not so cramped but thence               20
One sees the pulpit o' the epistle-side,
And somewhat of the choir, those silent seats,
And up into the aery dome where live
The angels, and a sunbeam's sure to lurk:
And I shall fill my slab of basalt there,
And 'neath my tabernacle take my rest,
With those nine columns round me, two and two,
The odd one at my feet where Anselm stands:
Peach-blossom marble all, the rare, the ripe
As fresh-poured red wine of a mighty pulse.                   30

— Old Gandolf with his paltry onion-stone,
Put me where I may look at him! True peach,
Rosy and flawless: how I earned the prize!
Draw close: that conflagration of my church
— What then? So much was saved if aught were missed!
My sons, ye would not be my death? Go dig
The white-grape vineyard where the oil-press stood,
Drop water gently till the surface sink,
And if ye find . . . Ah God, I know not, I! . . .
Bedded in store of rotten fig-leaves soft,         40
And corded up in a tight olive-frail,
Some lump, ah God, of *lapis lazuli*,
Big as a Jew's head cut off at the nape,
Blue as a vein o'er the Madonna's breast . . .
Sons, all have I bequeathed you, villas, all,
That brave Frascati villa with its bath,
So, let the blue lump poise between my knees,
Like God the Father's globe on both his hands
Ye worship in the Jesu Church so gay,
For Gandolf shall not choose but see and burst!    50
Swift as a weaver's shuttle fleet our years:
Man goeth to the grave, and where is he?
Did I say basalt for my slab, sons? Black —
'T was ever antique-black I meant! How else
Shall ye contrast my frieze to come beneath?
The bas-relief in bronze ye promised me,
Those Pans and Nymphs ye wot of, and perchance
Some tripod, thyrsus, with a vase or so,
The Saviour at his sermon on the mount,
Saint Praxed in a glory, and one Pan        60
Ready to twitch the Nymph's last garment off,
And Moses with the tables . . . but I know
Ye mark me not! What do they whisper thee,
Child of my bowels, Anselm? Ah, ye hope
To revel down my villas while I gasp
Bricked o'er with beggar's mouldy travertine
Which Gandolf from his tomb-top chuckles at!
Nay, boys, ye love me — all of jasper, then!
'T is jasper ye stand pledged to, lest I grieve.
My bath must needs be left behind, alas!     70

One block, pure green as a pistachio-nut,
There's plenty jasper somewhere in the world –
And have I not Saint Praxed's ear to pray
Horses for ye, and brown Greek manuscripts,
And mistresses with great smooth marbly limbs?
– That's if ye carve my epitaph aright,
Choice Latin, picked phrase, Tully's every word,
No gaudy ware like Gandolf's second line –
Tully, my masters? Ulpian serves his need
And then how I shall lie through centuries,                80
And hear the blessed mutter of the mass,
And see God made and eaten all day long,
And feel the steady candle-flame, and taste
Good strong thick stupefying incense-smoke!
For as I lie here, hours of the dead night,
Dying in state and by such slow degrees,
I fold my arms as if they clasped a crook,
And stretch my feet forth straight as stone can point,
And let the bedclothes, for a mortcloth, drop
Into great laps and folds of sculptor's-work:            90
And as yon tapers dwindle, and strange thoughts
Grow, with a certain humming in my ears,
About the life before I lived this life,
And this life too, popes, cardinals and priests,
Saint Praxed at his sermon on the mount,
Your tall pale mother with her talking eyes,
And new-found agate urns as fresh as day,
And marble's language, Latin pure, discreet,
– Aha, ELUCESCEBAT quoth our friend?
No Tully, said I, Ulpian at the best!                     100
Evil and brief hath been my pilgrimage.
All *lapis*, all, sons! Else I give the Pope
My villas! Will ye ever eat my heart?
Ever your eyes were as a lizard's quick,
They glitter like your mother's for my soul,
Or ye would heighten my impoverished frieze,
Piece out its starved design, and fill my vase
With grapes, and add a vizor and a Term,
And to the tripod ye would tie a lynx
That in his struggle throws the thyrsus down,             110

To comfort me on my entablature
Whereon I am to lie till I must ask
'Do I live, am I dead?' There, leave me, there!
For ye have stabbed me with ingratitude
To death – ye wish it – God, ye wish it! Stone –
Gritstone, a-crumble! Clammy squares which sweat
As if the corpse they keep were oozing through –
And no more *lapis* to delight the world!
Well go! I bless ye. Fewer tapers there,
But in a row: and, going, turn your backs          120
– Ay, like departing altar-ministrants,
And leave me in my church, the church for peace,
That I may watch at leisure if he leers –
Old Gandolf, at me, from his onion-stone,
As still he envied me, so fair she was!

# Meeting at Night

### 1

The grey sea and the long black land;
And the yellow half-moon large and low;
And the startled little waves that leap
In fiery ringlets from their sleep,
As I gain the cove with pushing prow,
And quench its speed i' the slushy sand.

### 2

Then a mile of warm sea-scented beach;
Three fields to cross till a farm appears;
A tap at the pane, the quick sharp scratch
And blue spurt of a lighted match,
And a voice less loud, thro' its joys and fears,    10
Than the two hearts beating each to each!

# Parting at Morning

Round the cape of a sudden came the sea,
And the sun looked over the mountain's rim –
And straight was a path of gold for him,
And the need of a world of men for me.

# Fra Lippo Lippi

I am poor brother Lippo, by your leave!
You need not clap your torches to my face.
Zooks, what's to blame? you think you see a monk!
What, 't is past midnight, and you go the rounds,
And here you catch me at an alley's end
Where sportive ladies leave their doors ajar?
The Carmine's my cloister: hunt it up,
Do, – harry out, if you must show your zeal,
Whatever rat, there, haps on his wrong hole,
And nip each softling of a wee white mouse,                          10
Weke, weke, that's crept to keep him company!
Aha, you know your betters! Then, you'll take
Your hand away that's fiddling on my throat,
And please to know me likewise. Who am I?
Why, one, sir, who is lodging with a friend
Three streets off – he's a certain . . . how d' ye call?
Master – a . . . Cosimo of the Medici,
I' the house that caps the corner. Boh! you were best!
Remember and tell me, the day you're hanged,
How you affected such a gullet's-gripe!                              20
But you, sir, it concerns you that your knaves
Pick up a manner nor discredit you:
Zooks, are we pilchards, that they sweep the streets
And count fair prize what comes into their net?
He's Judas to a tittle, that man is!
Just such a face! Why, sir, you make amends.
Lord, I'm not angry! Bid your hangdogs go
Drink out this quarter-florin to the health
Of the munificent House that harbours me
(And many more beside, lads! more beside!)                           30
And all's come square again. I'd like his face –
His, elbowing on his comrade in the door
With the pike and lantern, – for the slave that holds
John Baptist's head a-dangle by the hair
With one hand ('Look you, now,' as who should say)

And his weapon in the other, yet unwiped!
It's not your chance to have a bit of chalk,
A wood-coal or the like? or you should see!
Yes, I'm the painter, since you style me so.
What, brother Lippo's doings, up and down,                    40
You know them and they take you? like enough!
I saw the proper twinkle in your eye –
Tell you, I liked your looks at very first.
Let's sit and set things straight now, hip to haunch.
Here's spring come, and the nights one makes up bands
To roam the town and sing out carnival,
And I've been three weeks shut within my mew,
A-painting for the great man, saints and saints
And saints again. I could not paint all night –
Ouf! I leaned out of window for fresh air.                    50
There came a hurry of feet and little feet,
A sweep of lute-strings, laughs, and whifts of song,–
*Flower o' the broom,*
*Take away love, and our earth is a tomb!*
*Flower o' the quince,*
*I let Lisa go, and what good in life since?*
*Flower o' the thyme* – and so on. Round they went.
Scarce had they turned the corner when a titter
Like the skipping of rabbits by moonlight, – three slim shapes –
And a face that looked up . . . zooks, sir, flesh and blood,    60
That's all I'm made of! Into shreds it went,
Curtain and counterpane and coverlet,
All the bed-furniture – a dozen knots,
There was a ladder! Down I let myself,
Hands and feet, scrambling somehow, and so dropped,
And after them. I came up with the fun
Hard by Saint Laurence, hail fellow, well met,–
*Flower o' the rose,*
*If I've been merry, what matter who knows?*
And so as I was stealing back again                           70
To get to bed and have a bit of sleep
Ere I rise up to-morrow and go work
On Jerome knocking at his poor old breast
With his great round stone to subdue the flesh,
You snap me of the sudden. Ah, I see!

Though your eye twinkles still, you shake your head –
Mine's shaved – a monk, you say – the sting's in that!
If Master Cosimo announced himself,
Mum's the word naturally; but a monk!
Come, what am I a beast for? tell us, now!                        80
I was a baby when my mother died
And father died and left me in the street.
I starved there, God knows how, a year or two
On fig-skins, melon-parings, rinds and shucks,
Refuse and rubbish. One fine frosty day,
My stomach being empty as your hat,
The wind doubled me up and down I went.
Old Aunt Lapaccia trussed me with one hand,
(Its fellow was a stinger as I knew)
And so along the wall, over the bridge,                           90
By the straight cut to the convent. Six words there,
While I stood munching my first bread that month:
'So, boy, you're minded,' quoth the good fat father
Wiping his own mouth, 't was refection-time, –
'To quit this very miserable world?
Will you renounce' . . . The mouthful of bread? thought I;
By no means! Brief, they made a monk of me;
I did renounce the world, its pride and greed,
Palace, farm, villa, shop and banking-house,
Trash, such as these poor devils of Medici                        100
Have given their hearts to – all at eight years old.
Well, sir, I found in time, you may be sure,
'T was not for nothing – the good bellyful,
The warm serge and the rope that goes all round,
And day-long blessed idleness beside!
'Let's see what the urchin's fit for' – that came next.
Not overmuch their way, I must confess.
Such a to-do! They tried me with their books:
Lord, they'd have taught me Latin in pure waste!
*Flower o' the clove,*                                            110
*All the Latin I construe is, 'amo' I love!*
But, mind you, when a boy starves in the streets
Eight years together, as my fortune was,
Watching folk's faces to know who will fling
The bit of half-stripped grape-bunch he desires,

And who will curse or kick him for his pains, –
Which gentleman processional and fine,
Holding a candle to the Sacrament,
Will wink and let him lift a plate and catch
The droppings of the wax to sell again,                      120
Or holla for the Eight and have him whipped, –
How say I? – nay, which dog bites, which lets drop
His bone from the heap of offal in the street, –
Why, soul and sense of him grow sharp alike,
He learns the look of things, and none the less
For admonition from the hunger-pinch.
I had a store of such remarks, be sure,
Which, after I found leisure, turned to use:
I drew men's faces on my copy-books,
Scrawled them within the antiphonary's marge,              130
Joined legs and arms to the long music-notes,
Found eyes and nose and chin for A.s and B.s,
And made a string of pictures of the world
Betwixt the ins and outs of verb and noun,
On the wall, the bench, the door. The monks looked black.
'Nay,' quoth the Prior, 'turn him out, d' ye say?
In no wise. Lose a crow and catch a lark.
What if at last we get our man of parts,
We Carmelites, like those Camaldolese
And Preaching Friars, to do our church up fine              140
And put the front on it that ought to be!'
And hereupon he bade me daub away.
Thank you! my head being crammed, the walls a blank,
Never was such prompt disemburdening.
First, every sort of monk, the black and white,
I drew them, fat and lean: then, folk at church,
From good old gossips waiting to confess
Their cribs of barrel-droppings, candle-ends, –
To the breathless fellow at the altar-foot,
Fresh from his murder, safe and sitting there              150
With the little children round him in a row
Of admiration, half for his beard and half
For that white anger of his victim's son
Shaking a fist at him with one fierce arm,
Signing himself with the other because of Christ

(Whose sad face on the cross sees only this
After the passion of a thousand years)
Till some poor girl, her apron o'er her head,
(Which the intense eyes looked through) came at eve
On tiptoe, said a word, dropped in a loaf,     160
Her pair of earrings and a bunch of flowers
(The brute took growling), prayed, and so was gone.
I painted all, then cried "tis ask and have;
Choose, for more's ready!' – laid the ladder flat,
And showed my covered bit of cloister-wall
The monks closed in a circle and praised loud
Till checked, taught what to see and not to see,
Being simple bodies, – 'That's the very man!
Look at the boy who stoops to pat the dog!
That woman's like the Prior's niece who comes     170
To care about his asthma: it's the life!'
But there my triumph's straw-fire flared and funked;
Their betters took their turn to see and say:
The Prior and the learned pulled a face
And stopped all that in no time. 'How? what's here?
Quite from the mark of painting, bless us all!
Faces, arms, legs and bodies like the true
As much as pea and pea! it's devil's-game!
Your business is not to catch men with show,
With homage to the perishable clay,     180
But lift them over it, ignore it all,
Make them forget there's such a thing as flesh.
Your business is to paint the souls of men –
Man's soul, and it's a fire, smoke . . . no, it's not . . .
It's vapour done up like a new-born babe –
(In that shape when you die it leaves your mouth)
It's . . . well, what matters talking, it's the soul!
Give us no more of body than shows soul!
Here's Giotto, with his Saint a-praising God,
That sets us praising, – why not stop with him?     190
Why put all thoughts of praise out of our head
With wonder at lines, colours, and what not?
Paint the soul, never mind the legs and arms!
Rub all out, try at it a second time.
Oh, that white smallish female with the breasts,

She's just my niece . . . Herodias, I would say, –
Who went and danced and got men's heads cut off!
Have it all out!' Now, is this sense, I ask?
A fine way to paint soul, by painting body
So ill, the eye can't stop there, must go further          200
And can't fare worse! Thus, yellow does for white
When what you put for yellow's simply black,
And any sort of meaning looks intense
When all beside itself means and looks nought.
Why can't a painter lift each foot in turn,
Left foot and right foot, go a double step,
Make his flesh liker and his soul more like,
Both in their order? Take the prettiest face,
The Prior's niece . . . patron-saint – is it so pretty
You can't discover if it means hope, fear,                 210
Sorrow or joy? won't beauty go with these?
Suppose I've made her eyes all right and blue,
Can't I take breath and try to add life's flash,
And then add soul and heighten them threefold?
Or say there's beauty with no soul at all –
(I never saw it – put the case the same –)
If you get simple beauty and nought else,
You get about the best thing God invents:
That's somewhat: and you'll find the soul you have missed,
Within yourself, when you return Him thanks!               220
'Rub all out!' Well, well, there's my life, in short,
And so the thing has gone on ever since.
I'm grown a man no doubt, I've broken bounds:
You should not take a fellow eight years old
And make him swear to never kiss the girls.
I'm my own master, paint now as I please –
Having a friend, you see, in the Corner-house!
Lord, it's fast holding by the rings in front –
Those great things serve more purposes than just
To plant a flag in, or tie up a horse!                     230
And yet the old schooling sticks, the old grave eyes
Are peeping o'er my shoulder as I work,
The heads shake still – 'It's art's decline, my son!
You're not of the true painters, great and old;
Brother Angelico's the man, you'll find;

Brother Lorenzo stands his single peer:
Fag on at flesh, you'll never make the third!'
*Flower o' the pine,*
*You keep your mistr . . . manners, and I'll stick to mine!*
I'm not the third, then: bless us, they must know!                    240
Don't you think they're the likeliest to know,
They with their Latin? So, I swallow my rage,
Clench my teeth, suck my lips in tight, and paint
To please them – sometimes do and sometimes don't;
For, doing most, there's pretty sure to come
A turn, some warm eve finds me at my saints –
A laugh, a cry, the business of the world –
(*Flower o' the peach,*
*Death for us all, and his own life for each!*)
And my whole soul revolves, the cup runs o'er,                       250
The world and life's too big to pass for a dream,
And I do these wild things in sheer despite,
And play the fooleries you catch me at,
In pure rage! The old mill-horse, out at grass
After hard years, throws up his stiff heels so,
Although the miller does not preach to him
The only good of grass is to make chaff.
What would men have? Do they like grass or no –
May they or mayn't they? all I want's the thing
Settled for ever one way. As it is,
You tell too many lies and hurt yourself:                            260
You don't like what you only like too much,
You do like what, if given you at your word,
You find abundantly detestable.
For me, I think I speak as I was taught –
I always see the garden and God there
A-making man's wife: and, my lesson learned,
The value and significance of flesh,
I can't unlearn ten minutes afterwards,

     You understand me: I'm a beast, I know.                          270
But see, now – why, I see as certainly
As that the morning-star's about to shine,
What will hap some day. We've a youngster here
Comes to our convent, studies what I do,
Slouches and stares and lets no atom drop:

His name is Guidi – he'll not mind the monks –
They call him Hulking Tom, he lets them talk –
He picks my practice up – he'll paint apace,
I hope so – though I never live so long,
I know what's sure to follow. You be judge!                    280
You speak no Latin more than I, belike,
However, you're my man, you've seen the world
– The beauty and the wonder and the power,
The shapes of things, their colours, lights and shades,
Changes, surprises, – and God made it all!
– For what? Do you feel thankful, ay or no,
For this fair town's face, yonder river's line,
The mountain round it and the sky above,
Much more the figures of man, woman, child,
These are the frame to? What's it all about?                  290
To be passed over, despised? or dwelt upon,
Wondered at? oh, this last of course! – you say.
But why not do as well as say, – paint these
Just as they are, careless what comes of it?
God's works – paint anyone, and count it crime
To let a truth slip. Don't object, 'His works
Are here already; nature is complete:
Suppose you reproduce her – (which you can't)
There's no advantage! you must beat her, then.'
For, don't you mark? we're made so that we love           300
First when we see them painted, things we have passed
Perhaps a hundred times nor cared to see;
And so they are better, painted – better to us,
Which is the same thing. Art was given for that;
God uses us to help each other so,
Lending our minds out. Have you noticed, now,
Your cullion's hanging face? A bit of chalk,
And trust me but you should, though! How much more,
If I drew higher things with the same truth!
That were to take the Prior's pulpit-place,                    310
Interpret God to all of you! Oh, oh,
It makes me mad to see what men shall do
And we in our graves! This world's no blot for us,
Nor blank; it means intensely, and means good:
To find its meaning is my meat and drink.

'Ay, but you don't so instigate to prayer!'
Strikes in the Prior: 'when your meaning's plain
It does not say to folk – remember matins,
Or, mind you fast next Friday!' Why, for this
What need of art at all? A skull and bones,                    320
Two bits of stick nailed crosswise, or, what's best,
A bell to chime the hour with, does as well.
I painted a Saint Laurence six months since
At Prato, splashed the fresco in fine style:
'How looks my painting, now the scaffold's down?'
I ask a brother: 'Hugely,' he returns –
'Already not one phiz of your three slaves
Who turn the Deacon off his toasted side,
But's scratched and prodded to our heart's content,
The pious people have so eased their own                       330
With coming to say prayers there in a rage:
We get on fast to see the bricks beneath.
Expect another job this time next year,
For pity and religion grow i' the crowd –
Your painting serves its purpose!' Hang the fools!
– That is – you'll not mistake an idle word
Spoke in a huff by a poor monk, God wot,
Tasting the air this spicy night which turns
The unaccustomed head like Chianti wine!
Oh, the church knows! don't misreport me, now!                 340
It's natural a poor monk out of bounds
Should have his apt word to excuse himself:
And hearken how I plot to make amends.
I have bethought me: I shall paint a piece
. . . There's for you! Give me six months, then go, see
Something in Sant' Ambrogio's . . (Bless the nuns!
They want a cast o' my office). I shall paint
God in the midst, Madonna and her babe,
Ringed by a bowery, flowery angel-brood,
Lilies and vestments and white faces, sweet                    350
As puff on puff of grated orris-root
When ladies crowd to Church at midsummer.
And then i' the front, of course a saint or two –
Saint John, because he saves the Florentines,
Saint Ambrose, who puts down in black and white

The convent's friends and gives them a long day,
And Job, I must have him there past mistake,
The man of Uz (and Us without the z,
Painters who need his patience). Well, all these
Secured at their devotion, up shall come                     360
Out of a corner when you least expect,
As one by a dark stair into a great light,
Music and talking, who but Lippo! I! –
Mazed, motionless and moonstruck – I'm the man!
Back I shrink – what is this I see and hear?
I, caught up with my monk's-things by mistake,
My old serge gown and rope that goes all round,
I, in this presence, this pure company!
Where's a hole, where's a corner for escape?
Then steps a sweet angelic slip of a thing                   370
Forward, puts out a soft palm – 'Not so fast!'
– Addresses the celestial presence, 'nay –
He made you and devised you, after all,
Though he's none of you! Could Saint John there draw –
His camel-hair make up a painting-brush?
We come to brother Lippo for all that,
Iste perfecit opus!' So, all smile –
I shuffle sideways with my blushing face
Under the cover of a hundred wings
Thrown like a spread of kirtles when you're gay              380
And play hot cockles, all the doors being shut,
Till, wholly unexpected, in there pops
The hothead husband! Thus I scuttle off
To some safe bench behind, not letting go
The palm of her, the little lily thing
That spoke the good word for me in the nick,
Like the Prior's niece . . . Saint Lucy I would say.
And so all's saved for me, and for the church
A pretty picture gained. Go, six months hence!
Your hand, sir, and good-bye: no lights, no lights!          390
The street's hushed, and I know my own way back –
Don't fear me! There's the grey beginning. Zooks!

# A Toccata of Galuppi's

### 1

Oh Galuppi, Baldassaro, this is very sad to find!
I can hardly misconceive you; it would prove me deaf and blind;
But although I take your meaning, 'tis with such a heavy mind!

### 2

Here you come with your old music, and here's all the good it
    brings.
What, they lived once thus at Venice where the merchants were
    the kings,
Where Saint Mark's is, where the Doges used to wed the sea with
    rings?

### 3

Ay, because the sea's the street there; and 't is arched by . . .
    what you call
. . . Shylock's bridge with houses on it, where they kept the
    carnival:
I was never out of England – it's as if I saw it all.

### 4

Did young people take their pleasure when the sea was warm in
    May?                                                                          10
Balls and masks begun at midnight, burning ever to midday,
When they made up fresh adventures for the morrow, do you
    say?

### 5

Was a lady such a lady, cheeks so round and lips so red, –
On her neck the small face buoyant, like a bell-flower on its bed,
O'er the breast's superb abundance where a man might base his
    head?

6

Well, and it was graceful of them – they'd break talk off and
    afford
– She, to bite her mask's black velvet – he, to finger on his sword,
While you sat and played Toccatas, stately at the clavichord?


7

What? Those lesser thirds so plaintive, sixths diminished, sigh on
    sigh,
Told them something? Those suspensions, those solutions – 'Must
    we die?'                                                        20
Those commiserating sevenths – 'Life might last! we can but try!'


8

'Were you happy?' – 'Yes.' – 'And are you still as happy?' – 'Yes.
And you?'
– 'Then, more kisses!' – 'Did I stop them, when a
    million seemed so few?'
Hark, the dominant's persistence till it must be answered to!


9

So, an octave struck the answer. Oh, they praised you, I dare say!
'Brave Galuppi! that was music! good alike at grave and gay!
I can always leave off talking when I hear a master play?'


10

Then they left you for their pleasure: till in due time, one by one,
Some with lives that came to nothing, some with deeds as well
    undone,
Death stepped tacitly and took them where they never see the
    sun.                                                           30


11

But when I sit down to reason, think to take my stand nor
    swerve,
While I triumph o'er a secret wrung from nature's close reserve,
In you come with your cold music till I creep thro' every nerve.

12

Yes, you, like a ghostly cricket, creaking where a house was
   burned:
'Dust and ashes, dead and done with, Venice spent what Venice
   earned.
The soul, doubtless, is immortal – where a soul can be discerned.

13

'Yours for instance: you know physics, something of geology,
Mathematics are your pastime; souls shall rise in their degree;
Butterflies may dread extinction, – you'll not die, it cannot be!

14

As for Venice and her people, merely born to bloom and drop,   40
Here on earth they bore their fruitage, mirth and folly were the
   crop:
What of soul was left, I wonder, when the kissing had to stop?

15

Dust and ashes!' So you creak it, and I want the heart to scold.
Dear dead women, with such hair, too – what's become of all the
   gold
Used to hang and brush their bosoms? I feel chilly and grown old.

# Any Wife to Any Husband

### 1

My love, this is the bitterest, that thou –
Who art all truth, and who dost love me now
  As thine eyes say, as thy voice breaks to say –
Shouldst love so truly, and couldst love me still
A whole long life through, had but love its will,
  Would death that leads me from thee brook delay.

### 2

I have but to be by thee, and thy hand
Will never let mine go, nor heart withstand
  The beating of my heart to reach its place.
When shall I look for thee and feel thee gone?          10
When cry for the old comfort and find none?
  Never, I know! Thy soul is in thy face.

### 3

Oh, I should fade – 't is willed so! Might I save,
Gladly I would, whatever beauty gave
  Joy to thy sense, for that was precious too.
It is not to be granted. But the soul
Whence the love comes, all ravage leaves that whole;
  Vainly the flesh fades; soul makes all things new.

### 4

It would not be because my eye grew dim
Thou couldst not find the love there, thanks to Him          20
  Who never is dishonoured in the spark
He gave us from his fire of fires, and bade
Remember whence it sprang, nor be afraid
  While that burns on, though all the rest grow dark.

### 5

So, how thou wouldst be perfect, white and clean
Outside as inside, soul and soul's demesne

Alike, this body given to show it by!
Oh, three-parts through the worst of life's abyss,
What plaudits from the next world after this,
    Couldst thou repeat a stroke and gain the sky!          30


### 6

And is it not the bitterer to think
That, disengage our hands and thou wilt sink
    Although thy love was love in very deed?
I know that nature! Pass a festive day
Thou dost not throw its relic-flower away
    Nor bid its music's loitering echo speed.


### 7

Thou let'st the stranger's glove lie where it fell;
If old things remain old things all is well,
    For thou art grateful as becomes man best:
And hadst thou only heard me play one tune,          40
Or viewed me from a window, not so soon
    With thee would such things fade as with the rest.


### 8

I seem to see! We meet and part; 't is brief;
The book I opened keeps a folded leaf,
    The very chair I sat on, breaks the rank;
That is a portrait of me on the wall –
Three lines, my face comes at so slight a call:
    And for all this, one little hour to thank!


### 9

But now, because the hour through years was fixed,
Because our inmost beings met and mixed,          50
    Because thou once hast loved me – wilt thou dare
Say to thy soul and Who may list beside,
'Therefore she is immortally my bride;
    Chance cannot change my love, nor time impair.


### 10

So, what if in the dusk of life that's left,
I, a tired traveller of my sun bereft,

Look from my path when, mimicking the same,
The fire-fly glimpses past me, come and gone?
– Where was it till the sunset? where anon
   It will be at the sunrise! What's to blame?'        60

### 11

Is it so helpful to thee? Canst thou take
The mimic up, nor, for the true thing's sake,
   Put gently by such efforts at a beam?
Is the remainder of the way so long,
Thou need'st the little solace, thou the strong?
   Watch out thy watch, let weak ones doze and dream!

### 12

– Ah, but the fresher faces! 'Is it true,'
Thou'lt ask, 'some eyes are beautiful and new?
   Some hair, – how can one choose but grasp such wealth?
And if a man would press his lips to lips        70
Fresh as the wilding hedge-rose-cup there slips
   The dew-drop out of, must it be by stealth?

### 13

It cannot change the love still kept for Her,
More than if such a picture I prefer
   Passing a day with, to a room's bare side:
The painted form takes nothing she possessed,
Yet, while the Titian's Venus lies at rest,
   A man looks. Once more, what is there to chide?'

### 14

So must I see, from where I sit and watch,
My own self sell myself, my hand attach        80
   Its warrant to the very thefts from me –
Thy singleness of soul that made me proud.
Thy purity of heart I loved aloud,
   Thy man's-truth I was bold to bid God see!

### 15

Love so, then, if thou wilt! Give all thou canst
Away to the new faces – disentranced,

(Say it and think it) obdurate no more:
Re-issue looks and words from the old mint,
Pass them afresh, no matter whose the print
   Image and superscription once they bore!      90


### 16

Re-coin thyself and give it them to spend, –
It all comes to the same thing at the end,
   Since mine thou wast, mine art and mine shalt be,
Faithful or faithless, sealing up the sum
Or lavish of my treasure, thou must come
   Back to the heart's place here I keep for thee!


### 17

Only, why should it be with strain at all?
Why must I, 'twixt the leaves of coronal,
   Put any kiss of pardon on thy brow?
Why need the other women know so much,      100
And talk together, 'Such the look and such
   The smile he used to love with, then as now!'


### 18

Might I die last and show thee! Should I find
Such hardship in the few years left behind,
   If free to take and light my lamp, and go
Into thy tomb, and shut the door and sit,
Seeing thy face on those four sides of it
   The better that they are so blank, I know!


### 19

Why, time was what I wanted, to turn o'er
Within my mind each look, get more and more     110
   By heart each word, too much to learn at first;
And join thee all the fitter for the pause
'Neath the low doorway's lintel. That were cause
   For lingering, though thou calledst, if I durst!


### 20

And yet thou art the nobler of us two:
What dare I dream of, that thou canst not do,

Outstripping my ten small steps with one stride?
I'll say then, here's a trial and a task –
Is it to bear? – if easy, I'll not ask:
   Though love fail, I can trust on in thy pride.          120


21

Pride? – when those eyes forestall the life behind
The death I have to go through! – when I find,
   Now that I want thy help most, all of thee!
What did I fear? Thy love shall hold me fast
Until the little minute's sleep is past
   And I wake saved. – And yet it will not be!

# Mesmerism

### 1

All I believed is true!
    I am able yet
    All I want to get
By a method as strange as new:
Dare I trust the same to you?

### 2

If at night, when the doors are shut,
    And the wood-worm picks,
    And the death-watch ticks,
And the bar has a flag of smut,
And a cat's in the water-butt –        10

### 3

And the socket floats and flares,
    And the house-beams groan,
    And a foot unknown
Is surmised on the garret-stairs,
And the locks slip unawares –

### 4

And the spider, to serve his ends,
    By a sudden thread,
    Arms and legs outspread,
On the table's midst descends,
Comes to find, God knows what friends! –    20

### 5

If since eve drew in, I say,
    I have sate and brought
    (So to speak) my thought
To bear on the woman away,
Till I felt my hair turn grey –

### 6

Till I seemed to have and hold
    In the vacancy
    'Twixt the wall and me,
From the hair-plait's chestnut gold
To the foot in its muslin fold –                              30

### 7

Have and hold, then and there,
    Her, from head to foot,
    Breathing and mute,
Passive and yet aware,
In the grasp of my steady stare –

### 8

Hold and have, there and then,
    All her body and soul
    That completes my Whole,
All that women add to men,
In the clutch of my steady ken –                              40

### 9

Having and holding, till
    I imprint her fast
    On the void at last
As the sun does whom he will
By the calotypist's skill –

### 10

Then, – if my heart's strength serve,
    And through all and each
    Of the veils I reach
To her soul and never swerve,
Knitting an iron nerve –                              50

### 11

Commanding that to advance
    And inform the shape
    Which has made escape
And before my countenance
Answers me glance for glance –

### 12

I, still with a gesture fit
    Of my hands that best
    Do my soul's behest,
Pointing the power from it,
While myself do steadfast sit –                    60

### 13

Steadfast and still the same
    On my object bent
    While the hands give vent
To my ardour and my aim
And break into very flame –

### 14

Then, I reach, I must believe,
    Not her soul in vain,
    For to me again
It reaches, and past retrieve
Is wound in the toils I weave –                    70

### 15

And must follow as I require
    As befits a thrall,
    Bringing flesh and all,
Essence and earth-attire,
To the source of the tractile fire –

### 16

Till the house called hers, not mine,
    With a growing weight
    Seems to suffocate
If she break not its leaden line
And escape from its close confine –                80

### 17

Out of doors into the night!
    On to the maze
    Of the wild wood-ways,

Not turning to left or right
From the pathway, blind with sight –

### 18

Making thro' rain and wind
   O'er the broken shrubs,
    'Twixt the stems and stubs,
With a still composed strong mind,
Not a care for the world behind –                    90

### 19

Swifter and still more swift,
   As the crowding peace
    Doth to joy increase
In the wide blind eyes uplift,
Thro' the darkness and the drift!

### 20

While I – to the shape, I too
   Feel my soul dilate
    Nor a whit abate
And relax not a gesture due
As I see my belief come true –                    100

### 21

For there! have I drawn or no
   Life to that lip?
    Do my fingers dip
In a flame which again they throw
On the cheek that breaks a-glow?

### 22

Ha! was the hair so first?
   What, unfilleted,
    Made alive and spread
Through the void with a rich outburst,
Chestnut gold-interspersed!                    110

23

Like the doors of a casket-shrine,
    See, on either side,
    Her two arms divide
Till the heart betwixt makes sign,
Take me, for I am thine!

24

Now – now – the door is heard
    Hark! the stairs and near –
    Nearer – and here –
Now! and at call the third
She enters without a word.      120

25

On doth she march and on
    To the fancied shape –
    It is past escape
Herself, now – the dream is done
And the shadow and she are one.

26

First I will pray. Do Thou
    That ownest the soul,
    Yet wilt grant controul
To another nor disallow
For a time, restrain me now!      130

27

I admonish me while I may,
    Not to squander guilt,
    Since require Thou wilt
At my hand its price one day!
What the price is, who can say?

# 'Childe Roland to the Dark Tower Came'

[Note: (See Edgar's song in *Lear*)]

### 1

My first thought was, he lied in every word,
　　That hoary cripple, with malicious eye
　　Askance to watch the working of his lie
On mine, and mouth scarce able to afford
Suppression of the glee, that pursed and scored
　　Its edge, at one more victim gained thereby.

### 2

What else should he be set for, with his staff?
　　What, save to wayday with his lies, ensnare
　　All travellers who might find him posted there,
And ask the road? I guessed what skull-like laugh    10
Would break, what crutch 'gin write my epitaph
　　For pastime in the dusty thoroughfare,

### 3

If at his counsel I should turn aside
　　Into that ominous tract which, all agree,
　　Hides the Dark Tower. Yet acquiescingly
I did turn as he pointed: neither pride
Nor hope rekindling at the end descried,
　　So much as gladness that some end might be

### 4

For, what with my whole world-wide wandering,
　　What with my search drawn out thro' years, my hope    20
　　Dwindled into a ghost not fit to cope
With that obstreperous joy success would bring, –
I hardly tried now to rebuke the spring
　　My heart made, finding failure in its scope.

### 5

As when a sick man very near to death
  Seems dead indeed, and feels begin and end
  The tears and takes the farewell of each friend,
And hears one bid the other go, draw breath
Freelier outside, ('since all is o'er,' he saith,
  'And the blow fallen no grieving can amend')    30

### 6

While some discuss if near the other graves
  Be room enough for this, and when a day
  Suits best for carrying the corpse away,
With care about the banners, scarves and staves:
And still the man hears all, and only craves
  He may not shame such tender love and stay.

### 7

Thus, I had so long suffered in this quest,
  Heard failure prophesied so oft, been writ
  So many times among 'The Band' – to wit,
The knights who to the Dark Tower's search addressed    40
Their steps – that just to fail as they, seemed best,
  And all the doubt was now – should I be fit?

### 8

So, quiet as despair, I turned from him,
  That hateful cripple, out of his highway
  Into the path he pointed. All the day
Had been a dreary one at best, and dim
Was settling to its close, yet shot one grim
  Red leer to see the plain catch its estray.

### 9

For mark! no sooner was I fairly found
  Pledged to the plain, after a pace or two,    50
  Than, pausing to throw backward a last view
O'er the safe road, 't was gone; grey plain all round:
Nothing but plain to the horizon's bound.
  I might go on; nought else remained to do.

### 10

So, on I went. I think I never saw
  Such starved ignoble nature; nothing throve:
  For flowers – as well expect a cedar grove!
But cockle, spurge, according to their law
Might propagate their kind, with none to awe,
  You'd think; a burr had been a treasure-trove.      60

### 11

No! penury, inertness and grimace,
  In some strange sort, were the land's portion. 'See
  Or shut your eyes,' – said Nature peevishly –
'It nothing skills: I cannot help my case:
''T is the Last Judgment's fire must cure this place,
  Calcine its clods and set my prisoners free.'

### 12

If there pushed any ragged thistle-stalk
  Above its mates, the head was chopped; the bents
  Were jealous else. What made those holes and rents
In the dock's harsh swarth leaves, bruised as to baulk    70
All hope of greenness? 't is a brute must walk
  Pashing their life out, with a brute's intents.

### 13

As for the grass, it grew as scant as hair
  In leprosy; thin dry blades pricked the mud
  Which underneath looked kneaded up with blood.
One stiff blind horse, his every bone a-stare,
Stood stupefied, however he came there:
  Thrust out past service from the devil's stud!

### 14

Alive? he might be dead for aught I know,
  With that red gaunt and colloped neck a-strain,    80
  And shut eyes underneath the rusty mane;
Seldom went such grotesqueness with such woe;
I never saw a brute I hated so;
  He must be wicked to deserve such pain.

### 15

I shut my eyes and turned them on my heart.
　As a man calls for wine before he fights,
　I asked one draught of earlier, happier sights,
Ere fitly I could hope to play my part.
Think first, fight afterwards – the soldier's art:
　One taste of the old time sets all to rights.　　　90

### 16

Not it! I fancied Cuthbert's reddening face
　Beneath its garniture of curly gold,
　Dear fellow, till I almost felt him fold
An arm in mine to fix me to the place,
That way he used. Alas, one night's disgrace!
　Out went my heart's new fire and left it cold.

### 17

Giles then, the soul of honour – there he stands
　Frank as ten years ago when knighted first.
　What honest man should dare (he said) he durst.
Good – but the scene shifts – faugh! what hangman-hands　100
Pin to his breast a parchment? His own bands
　Read it. Poor traitor, spit upon and curst!

### 18

Better this present than a past like that;
　Back therefore to my darkening path again!
　No sound, no sight as far as eye could strain.
Will the night send a howlet or a bat?
I asked: when something on the dismal flat
　Came to arrest my thoughts and change their train.

### 19

A sudden little river crossed my path
　As unexpected as a serpent comes.　　　110
　No sluggish tide congenial to the glooms;
This, as it frothed by, might have been a bath
For the fiend's glowing hoof – to see the wrath
　Of its black eddy bespate with flakes and spumes.

### 20

So petty yet so spiteful! All along,
   Low scrubby alders kneeled down over it;
   Drenched willows flung them headlong in a fit
Of mute despair, a suicidal throng:
The river which had done them all the wrong,
   Whate'er that was, rolled by, deterred no whit.       120

### 21

Which, while I forded, – good saints, how I feared
   To set my foot upon a dead man's cheek,
   Each step, or feel the spear I thrust to seek
For hollows, tangled in his hair or beard!
– It may have been a water-rat I speared,
   But, ugh! it sounded like a baby's shriek.

### 22

Glad was I when I reached the other bank.
   Now for a better country. Vain presage!
   Who were the strugglers, what war did they wage,
Whose savage trample thus could pad the dank       130
Soil to a plash? Toads in a poisoned tank,
   Or wild cats in a red-hot iron cage –

### 23

The fight must so have seemed in that fell cirque.
   What penned them there, with all the plain to choose?
   No foot-print leading to that horrid mews,
None out of it. Mad brewage set to work
Their brains, no doubt, like galley-slaves the Turk
   Pits for his pastime, Christians against Jews.

### 24

And more than that – a furlong on – why, there!
   What bad use was that engine for, that wheel,      140
   Or brake, not wheel – that harrow fit to reel
Men's bodies out like silk? with all the air
Of Tophet's tool, on earth left unaware,
   Or brought to sharpen its rusty teeth of steel.

### 25

Then came a bit of stubbed ground, once a wood,
   Next a marsh, it would seem, and now mere earth
   Desperate and done with; (so a fool finds mirth,
Makes a thing and then mars it, till his mood
Changes and off he goes!) within a rood –
   Bog, clay and rubble, sand and stark black dearth.    150

### 26

Now blotches rankling, coloured gay and grim,
   Now patches where some leanness of the soil's
   Broke into moss or substances like boils;
Then came some palsied oak, a cleft in him
Like a distorted mouth that splits its rim
   Gaping at death, and dies while it recoils.

### 27

And just as far as ever from the end!
   Nought in the distance but the evening, nought
   To point my footstep further! At the thought,
A great black bird, Apollyon's bosom-friend,    160
Sailed past, nor beat his wide wing dragon-penned
   That brushed my cap – perchance the guide I sought.

### 28

For, looking up, aware I somehow grew,
   'Spite of the dusk, the plain had given place
   All round to mountains – with such name to grace
Mere ugly heights and heaps now stolen in view.
How thus they had surprised me, – solve it, you!
   How to get from them was no clearer case.

### 29

Yet half I seemed to recognize some trick
   Of mischief happened to me, God knows when –    170
   In a bad dream perhaps. Here ended, then,
Progress this way. When, in the very nick
Of giving up, one time more, came a click
   As when a trap shuts – you're inside the den!

### 30

Burningly it came on me all at once,
   This was the place! those two hills on the right,
   Crouched like two bulls locked horn in horn in fight;
While to the left, a tall scalped mountain . . . Dunce,
Dotard, a-dozing at the very nonce,
   After a life spent training for the sight!          180

### 31

What in the midst lay but the Tower itself?
   The round squat turret, blind as the fool's heart,
   Built of brown stone, without a counterpart
In the whole world. The tempest's mocking elf
Points to the shipman thus the unseen shelf
   He strikes on, only when the timbers start.

### 32

Not see? because of night perhaps? – why, day
   Came back again for that! before it left,
   The dying sunset kindled through a cleft:
The hills, like giants at a hunting, lay,          190
Chin upon hand, to see the game at bay, –
   'Now stab and end the creature – to the heft!'

### 33

Not hear? when noise was everywhere! it tolled
   Increasing like a bell. Names in my ears
   Of all the lost adventurers my peers, –
How such a one was strong, and such was bold,
And such was fortunate, yet each of old
   Lost, lost! one moment knelled the woe of years.

### 34

There they stood, ranged along the hill-sides, met
   To view the last of me, a living frame         200
   For one more picture! in a sheet of flame
I saw them and I knew them all. And yet
Dauntless the slug-horn to my lips I set,
   And blew. *'Childe Roland to the Dark Tower came.'*

# Bishop Blougram's Apology

No more wine? Then we'll push back chairs and talk.
A final glass for me, tho'; cool, i'faith!
We ought to have our Abbey back, you see.
It's different, preaching in basilicas,
And doing duty in some masterpiece
Like this of brother Pugin's, bless his heart!
I doubt if they're half baked, those chalk rosettes,
Ciphers and stucco-twiddlings everywhere;
It's just like breathing in a lime-kiln: eh?
These hot long ceremonies of our church          10
Cost us a little – oh, they pay the price,
You take me – amply pay it! Now, we'll talk.

So, you despise me, Mr Gigadibs.
No deprecation, – nay, I beg you, sir!
Beside 'tis our engagement: don't you know,
I promised, if you'd watch a dinner out,
We'd see truth dawn together? – truth that peeps
Over the glass's edge when dinner's done,
And body gets its sop and holds its noise
And leaves soul free a little. Now's the time –          20
'Tis break of day! You do despise me then.
And if I say, 'despise me,' – never fear –
I know you do not in a certain sense –
Not in my arm-chair for example: here,
I well imagine you respect my place
(Status, *entourage*, worldly circumstance)
Quite to its value – very much indeed
– Are up to the protesting eyes of you
In pride at being seated here for once –
You'll turn it to such capital account!          30
When somebody, through years and years to come,
Hints of the bishop, – names me – that's enough –
'Blougram? I knew him' – (into it you slide)
'Dined with him once, a Corpus Christi Day,

All alone, we two – he's a clever man –
And after dinner, – why, the wine you know, –
Oh, there was wine, and good! – what with the wine . . .
'Faith, we began upon all sorts of talk!
He's no bad fellow, Blougram – he had seen
Something of mine he relished – some review –                    40
He's quite above their humbug in his heart,
Half-said as much, indeed – the thing's his trade –
I warrant, Blougram's sceptical at times –
How otherwise? I liked him, I confess!'
    *Che ch'é*, my dear sir, as we say at Rome,
Don't you protest now! It's fair give and take;
You have had your turn and spoken your home-truths –
The hand's mine now, and here you follow suit.

    Thus much conceded, still the first fact stays –
You do despise me; your ideal of life                            50
Is not the bishop's – you would not be I –
You would like better to be Goethe, now,
Or Buonaparte – or, bless me, lower still,
Count D'Orsay, – so you did what you preferred,
Spoke as you thought, and, as you cannot help,
Believed or disbelieved, no matter what,
So long as on that point, what'er it was,
You loosed your mind, were whole and sole yourself.
– That, my ideal never can include,
Upon that element of truth and worth                             60
Never be based! for say they make me Pope
(They can't – suppose it for our argument)
Why, there I'm at my tether's end – I've reached
My height, and not a height which pleases you.
An unbelieving Pope won't do, you say.
It's like those eerie stories nurses tell,
Of how some actor played Death on a stage
With pasteboard crown, sham orb, and tinselled dart,
And called himself the monarch of the world,
Then going in the tire-room afterward                            70
Because the play was done, to shift himself,
Got touched upon the sleeve familiarly
The moment he had shut the closet door

By Death himself. Thus God might touch a Pope
At unawares, ask what his baubles mean,
And whose part he presumed to play just now?
Best be yourself, imperial, plain and true!

So, drawing comfortable breath again,
You weigh and find whatever more or less
I boast of my ideal realised                           80
Is nothing in the balance when opposed
To your ideal, your grand simple life,
Of which you will not realise one jot.
I am much, you are nothing; you would be all,
I would be merely much – you beat me there.

No, friend you do not beat me, – hearken why.
The common problem, yours, mine, every one's,
Is not to fancy what were fair in life
Provided it could be, – but, finding first
What may be, then find how to make it fair          90
Up to our means – a very different thing!
No abstract intellectual plan of life
Quite irrespective of life's plainest laws,
But one, a man, who is man and nothing more,
May lead within a world which (by your leave)
Is Rome or London – not Fool's-paradise.
Embellish Rome, idealise away,
Make Paradise of London if you can,
You're welcome, nay, you're wise.

                                    A simile!        100
We mortals cross the ocean of this world
Each in his average cabin of a life –
The best's not big, the worst yields elbow-room.
Now for our six months' voyage – how prepare?
You come on shipboard with a landsman's list
Of things he calls convenient – so they are!
An India screen is pretty furniture,
A piano-forte is a fine resource,
All Balzac's novels occupy one shelf,
The new edition fifty volumes long;                 110

And little Greek books with the funny type
They get up well at Leipsic fill the next –
Go on! slabbed marble, what a bath it makes!
And Parma's pride, the Jerome, let us add!
'Twere pleasant could Correggio's fleeting glow
Hang full in face of one where'er one roams,
Since he more than the others brings with him
Italy's self, – the marvellous Modenese!
Yet 'twas not on your list before, perhaps.
– Alas! friend, here's the agent . . . is't the name?          120
The captain, or whoever's master here –
You see him screw his face up; what's his cry
Ere you set foot on shipboard? 'Six feet square!'
If you won't understand what six feet mean,
Compute and purchase stores accordingly –
And if in pique because he overhauls
Your Jerome, piano and bath, you come on board
Bare – why you cut a figure at the first
While sympathetic landsmen see you off;
Not afterwards, when, long ere half seas o'er          130
You peep up from your utterly naked boards
Into some snug and well-appointed berth
Like mine, for instance (try the cooler jug –
Put back the other, but don't jog the ice)
And mortified you mutter 'Well and good –
He sits enjoying his sea-furniture –
'Tis stout and proper, and there's store of it,
Though I've the better notion, all agree,
Of fitting rooms up! hang the carpenter,
Neat ship-shape fixings and contrivances –          140
I would have brought my Jerome, frame and all!'
And meantime you bring nothing: never mind –
You've proved your artist-nature: what you don't,
You might bring, so despise me, as I say.

Now come, let's backward to the starting place.
See my way: we're two college friends, suppose –
Prepare together for our voyage, then,
Each note and check the other in his work, –

Here's mine, a bishop's outfit; criticise!
What's wrong? why won't you be a bishop too?          150

   Why, first, you don't believe, you don't and can't,
(Not statedly, that is, and fixedly
And absolutely and exclusively)
In any revelation called divine.
No dogmas nail your faith – and what remains
But say so, like the honest man you are?
First, therefore, overhaul theology!
Nay, I too, not a fool, you please to think,
Must find believing every whit as hard,
And if I do not frankly say as much,          160
The ugly consequence is clear enough.

   Now, wait, my friend: well, I do not believe –
If you'll accept no faith that is not fixed,
Absolute and exclusive, as you say.
(You're wrong – I mean to prove it in due time)
Meanwhile, I know where difficulties lie
I could not, cannot solve, nor ever shall,
So give up hope accordingly to solve –
(To you, and over the wine). Our dogmas then
With both of us, tho' in unlike degree,          170
Missing full credence – overboard with them!
I mean to meet you on your own premise –
Good, there go mine in company with yours!

   And now what are we? unbelievers both,
Calm and complete, determinately fixed
To-day, to-morrow, and for ever, pray?
You'll guarantee me that? Not so, I think.
In no-wise! all we've gained is, that belief,
As unbelief before, shakes us by fits,
Confounds us like its predecessor. Where's          180
The gain? how can we guard our unbelief,
Make it bear fruit to us? – the problem here.
Just when we are safest, there's a sunset-touch,
A fancy from a flower-bell, some one's death,
A chorus-ending from Euripides, –
And that's enough for fifty hopes and fears

As old and new at once at Nature's self,
To rap and knock and enter in our soul,
Take hands and dance there, a fantastic ring,
Round the ancient idol, on his base again, –       190
The grand Perhaps! we look on helplessly, –
There the old misgivings, crooked questions are –
This good God, – what he could do, if he would,
Would, if he could – then must have done long since:
If so, when, where, and how? Some way must be, –
Once feel about, and soon or late you hit
Some sense, in which it might be, after all.
Why not, 'The Way, the Truth, the Life?'

                    – That way
Over the mountain, which who stands upon
Is apt to doubt if it's indeed a road;       200
While if he views it from the waste itself,
Up goes the line there, plain from base to brow,
Not vague, mistakeable! what's a break or two
Seen from the unbroken desert either side?
And then (to bring in fresh philosophy)
What if the breaks themselves should prove at last
The most consummate of contrivances
To train a man's eye, teach him what is faith, –
And so we stumble at truth's very test?
What have we gained then by our unbelief       210
But a life of doubt diversified by faith,
For one of faith diversified by doubt?
We called the chess-board white, – we call it black.

   'Well,' you rejoin, 'the end's no worse, at least,
We've reason for both colours on the board.
Why not confess, then, where I drop the faith
And you the doubt, that I'm as right as you?'

   Because, friend, in the next place, this being so,
And both things even, – faith and unbelief
Left to a man's choice, – we'll proceed a step,      220
Returning to our image, which I like.

A man's choice, yes – but a cabin-passenger's –
The man made for the special life of the world –
Do you forget him? I remember though!
Consult our ship's conditions and you find
One and but one choice suitable to all,
The choice that you unluckily prefer
Turning things topsy-turvy – they or it
Going to the ground. Belief or unbelief
Bears upon life, determines its whole course,                   230
Begins at its beginning. See the world
Such as it is, – you made it not, nor I;
I mean to take it as it is, – and you
Not so you'll take it, – though you get nought else.
I know the special kind of life I like,
What suits the most of my idiosyncrasy,
Brings out the best of me and bears me fruit
In power, peace, pleasantness, and length of days.
I find that positive belief does this
For me, and unbelief, no whit of this.                          240
– For you, it does, however – that we'll try!
'Tis clear, I cannot lead my life, at least
Induce the world to let me peaceably,
Without declaring at the outset, 'Friends,'
I absolutely and peremptorily
Believe!' – I say faith is my waking life.
One sleeps, indeed, and dreams at intervals,
We know, but waking's the main point with us,
And my provision's for life's waking part.
Accordingly, I use heart, head and hands                        250
All day, I build, scheme, study and make friends;
And when night overtakes me, down I lie,
Sleep, dream a little, and get done with it,
The sooner the better, to begin afresh.
What's midnight's doubt before the dayspring's faith?
You, the philosopher, that disbelieve,
That recognise the night, give dreams their weight –
To be consistent you should keep your bed,
Abstain from healthy acts that prove you a man,
For fear you drowse perhaps at unawares!                        260
And certainly at night you'll sleep and dream,

Live through the day and bustle as you please.
And so you live to sleep as I to wake,
To unbelieve as I to still believe?
Well, and the common sense of the world calls you
Bed-ridden, – and its good things come to me.
Its estimation, which is half the fight,
That's the first cabin-comfort I secure –
The next . . . but you perceive with half an eye!
Come, come, it's best believing, if we can –                270
You can't but own that.

                              Next, concede again –
If once we choose belief, on all accounts
We can't be too decisive in our faith,
Conclusive and exclusive in its terms,
To suit the world which gives us the good things.
In every man's career are certain points
Whereon he dares not be indifferent;
The world detects him clearly, if he is,
As baffled at the game, and losing life.
He may care little or he may care much                       280
For riches, honour, pleasure, work, repose,
Since various theories of life and life's
Success are extant which might easily
Comport with either estimate of these,
And whoso chooses wealth or poverty,
Labour or quiet, is not judged a fool
Because his fellows would choose otherwise.
We let him choose upon his own account
So long as he's consistent with his choice.
But certain points, left wholly to himself,                  290
When once a man has arbitrated on,
We say he must succeed there or go hang.
Thus, he should wed the woman he loves most
Or needs most, whatsoe'er the love or need –
For he can't wed twice. Then, he must avouch
Or follow, at the least, sufficiently,
The form of faith his conscience holds the best,
Whate'er the process of conviction was.
For nothing can compensate his mistake

On such a point, the man himself being judge –        300
He cannot wed twice, nor twice lose his soul.

    Well now – there's one great form of Christian faith
I happened to be born in – which to teach
Was given me as I grew up, on all hands,
As best and readiest means of living by;
The same on examination being proved
The most pronounced moreover, fixed, precise
And absolute form of faith in the whole world –
Accordingly, most potent of all forms
For working on the world. Observe, my friend,        310
Such as you know me, I am free to say,
In these hard latter days which hamper one,
Myself, by no immoderate exercise
Of intellect and learning, and the tact
To let external forces work for me,
Bid the street's stones be bread and they are bread,
Bid Peter's creed, or, rather, Hildebrand's,
Exalt me o'er my fellows in the world
And make my life an ease and joy and pride,
It does so, – which for me's a great point gained,        320
Who have a soul and body that exact
A comfortable care in many ways.
There's power in me and will to dominate
Which I must exercise, they hurt me else:
In many ways I need mankind's respect,
Obedience, and the love that's born of fear:
While at the same time, there's a taste I have,
A toy of soul, a titillating thing,
Refuses to digest these dainties crude.
The naked life is gross till clothed upon:        330
I must take what men offer, with a grace
As though I would not, could I help it, take!
A uniform to wear though over-rich –
Something imposed on me, no choice of mine;
No fancy-dress worn for pure fashion's sake
And despicable therefore! now men kneel
And kiss my hand – of course the Church's hand.
Thus I am made, thus life is best for me,

And thus that it should be I have procured;
And thus it could not be another way,                      340
I venture to imagine.

                     You'll reply —
So far my choice, no doubt, is a success;
But were I made of better elements,
With nobler instincts, purer tastes, like you,
I hardly would account the thing success
Though it do all for me I say.

                    But, friend,
We speak of what is — not of what might be,
And how 'twere better if 'twere otherwise.
I am the man you see here plain enough —
Grant I'm a beast, why beasts must lead beasts' lives      350
Suppose I own at once to tail and claws —
The tailless man exceeds me; but being tailed
I'll lash out lion-fashion, and leave apes
To dock their stump and dress their haunches up.
My business is not to remake myself,
But make the absolute best of what God made.
Or — our first simile — though you proved me doomed
To a viler berth still, to the steerage-hole,
The sheep-pen or the pig-stye, I should strive
To make what use of each were possible;                    360
And as this cabin gets upholstery,
That hutch should rustle with sufficient straw.

   But, friend, I don't acknowledge quite so fast
I fail of all your manhood's lofty tastes
Enumerated so complacently.
On the mere ground that you forsooth can find
In this particular life I choose to lead
No fit provision for them. Can you not?
Say you, my fault is I address myself
To grosser estimators than I need,                         370
And that's no way of holding up the soul —
Which, nobler, needs men's praise perhaps, yet knows
One wise man's verdict outweights all the fools', —

Would like the two, but, forced to choose, takes that?
I pine among my million imbeciles
(You think) aware some dozen men of sense
Eye me and know me, whether I believe
In the last winking Virgin, as I vow,
And am a fool, or disbelieve in her
And am a knave, – approve in neither case,                    380
Withhold their voices though I look their way:
Like Verdi when, at his worst opera's end
(The thing they gave at Florence, – what's its name?)
While the mad houseful's plaudits near out-bang
His orchestra of salt-box, tongs and bones,
He looks through all the roaring and the wreaths
Where sits Rossini patient in his stall.

    Nay, friend, I meet you with an answer here –
For even your prime men who appraise their kind
Are men still, catch a thing within a thing,                  390
See more in a truth than the truth's simple self,
Confuse themselves. You see lads walk the street
Sixty the minute; what's to note in that?
You see one lad o'erstride a chimney-stack;
Him you must watch – he's sure to fall, yet stands!
Our interest's on the dangerous edge of things.
The honest thief, the tender murderer,
The superstitious atheist, demireps
That love and save their souls in new French books –
We watch while these in equilibrium keep                      400
The giddy line midway: one step aside,
They're classed and done with. I, then, keep the line
Before your sages, – just the men to shrink
From the gross weights, coarse scales, and labels broad
You offer their refinement. Fool or knave?
Why needs a bishop be a fool or knave?
When there's a thousand diamond weights between?
So I enlist them. Your picked Twelve, you'll find,
Profess themselves indignant, scandalised
At thus being held unable to explain                          410
How a superior man who disbelieves
May not believe as well: that's Schelling's way!

It's through my coming in the tail of time,
Nicking the minute with a happy tact.
Had I been born three hundred years ago
They'd say, 'What's strange? Blougram of course believes;'
And, seventy years since, 'disbelieves of course.'
But now, 'He may believe,; and yet, and yet
How can he?' – All eyes turn with interest.
Whereas, step off the line on either side –                      420
You, for example, clever to a fault,
The rough and ready man that write apace,
Read somewhat seldomer, think perhaps even less –
You disbelieve! Who wonders and who cares?
Lord-So-and-So – his coat bedropt with wax,
All Peter's chains about his waist, his back
Brave with the needlework of Noodledom,
Believes! Again, who wonders and who cares?
But I, the man of sense and learning too,
The able to think yet act, the this, the that,                  430
I, to believe at this late time of day!
Enough; you see, I need not fear contempt.

   – Except it's yours! admire me as these may,
You don't. But what at least do you admire?
Present your own perfections, your ideal,
Your pattern man for a minute – oh, make haste!
Is it Napoleon you would have us grow?
Concede the means; allow his head and hand,
(A large concession, clever as you are)
Good! – in our common primal element                            440
Of unbelief (we can't believe, you know –
We're still at that admission, recollect)
Where do you find – apart from, towering-o'er
The secondary temporary aims
Which satisfy the gross tastes you despise –
Where do you find his star? – his crazy trust
God knows through what or in what? it's alive
And shines and leads him and that's all we want.
Have we ought in our sober night shall point
Such ends as his were, and direct the means                     450
Of working out our purpose straight as his,

Nor bring a moment's trouble on success,
With after-care to justify the same?
– Be a Napoleon and yet disbelieve!
Why, the man's mad, friend, take his light away.
What's the vague good of the world for which you'd dare
With comfort to yourself blow millions up?
We neither of us see it! we do see
The blown-up millions – spatter of their brains
And writhing of their bowels and so forth,                460
In that bewildering entanglement
Of horrible eventualities
Past calculation to the end of time!
Can I mistake for some clear word of God
(Which were my ample warrant for it all)
His puff of hazy instincts, idle talk,
'The state, that's I,' quack-nonsense about kings,
And (when one beats the man to his last hold)
The vague idea of setting things to rights,
Policing people efficaciously,                470
More to their profit, most of all to his own;
The whole to end that dismallest of ends
By an Austrian marriage, cant to us the church,
And resurrection of the old *régime*.
Would I, who hope to live a dozen years,
Fight Austerlitz for reasons such and such?
No: for, concede me but the merest chance
Doubt may be wrong – there's judgment, life to come!
With just that chance, I dare not. Doubt proves right?
This present life is all? you offer me                480
Its dozen noisy years with not a chance
That wedding an Arch-Duchess, wearing lace,
And getting called by divers new-coined names,
Will drive off ugly thoughts and let me dine,
Sleep, read and chat in quiet as I like!
Therefore, I will not.

       Take another case;
Fit up the cabin yet another way.
What say you to the poet's? Shall we write
Hamlets, Othellos – make the world our own,

Without a risk to run of either sort?                               490
I can't! – to put the strongest reason first.
'But try,' you urge, 'the trying shall suffice:
The aim, if reached or not, makes great the life.
Try to be Shakspeare, leave the rest to fate!'
Spare my self-knowledge – there's no fooling me!
If I prefer remaining my poor self,
I say so not in self-dispraise but praise.
If I'm a Shakspeare, let the well alone –
Why should I try to be what now I am?
If I'm no Shakspeare, as too probable, –               500
His power and consciousness and self-delight
And all we want in common, shall I find –
Trying for ever? while on points of taste
Wherewith, to speak it humbly, he and I
Are dowered alike – I'll ask you, I or he,
Which in our two lives realises most?
Much, he imagined – somewhat, I possess.
He had the imagination; stick to that!
Let him say 'In the face of my soul's works
Your world is worthless and I touch it not               510
Lest I should wrong them' – I withdraw my plea.
But does he say so? look upon his life!
Himself, who only can, gives judgment there.
He leaves his towers and gorgeous palaces
To build the trimmest house in Stratford town;
Saves money, spends it, owns the worth of things,
Giulio Romano's pictures, Dowland's lute;
Enjoys a show, respects the puppets, too,
And none more, had he seen its entry once,
Than 'Pandulph, of fair Milan cardinal.'               520
Why then should I who play that personage,
The very Pandulph Shakspeare's fancy made,
Be told that had the poet chanced to start
From where I stand now (some degree like mine
Being just the goal he ran his race to reach)
He would have run the whole race back, forsooth,
And left being Pandulph, to begin write plays?
Ah, the earth's best can be but the earth's best!
Did Shakspeare live, he could but sit at home

And get himself in dreams the Vatican,                530
Greek busts, Venetian paintings, Roman walls,
And English books, none equal to his own,
Which I read, bound in gold, (he never did).
– Terni and Naples' bay and Gothard's top –
Eh, friend? I could not fancy one of these –
But, as I pour this claret, there they are –
I've gained them – crossed St Gothard last July
With ten mules to the carriage and a bed
Slung inside; is my hap the worse for that?
We want the same things, Shakspeare and myself,                540
And what I want, I have: he, gifted more,
Could fancy he too had it when he liked,
But not so thoroughly that if fate allowed
He would not have it also in my sense.
We play one game. I send the ball aloft
No less adroitly that of fifty strokes
Scarce five go o'er the wall so wide and high
Which sends them back to me: I wish and get.
He struck balls higher and with better skill,
But at a poor fence level with his head,                550
And hit – his Stratford house, a coat of arms,
Successful dealings in his grain and wool, –
While I receive heaven's incense in my nose
And style myself the cousin of Queen Bess.
Ask him, if this life's all, who wins the game?

Believe – and our whole argument breaks up.
Enthusiasm's the best thing, I repeat;
Only, we can't command it; fire and life
Are all, dead matter's nothing; we agree:
And be it a mad dream or God's very breath,                560
The fact's the same, – belief's fire once in us,
Makes of all else mere stuff to show itself.
We penetrate our life with such a glow
As fire lends wood and iron – this turns steel,
That burns to ash – all's one, fire proves its power
For good or ill, since men call flare success.
But paint a fire, it will not therefore burn.
Light one in me, I'll find it food enough!

Why, to be Luther – that's life to lead,
Imcomparably better than my own.                              570
He comes, reclaims God's earth for God, he says,
Sets up God's rule again by simple means,
Re-opens a shut book, and all is done.
He flared out in the flaring of mankind;
Such Luther's luck was – how shall such be mine?
If he succeeded, nothing's left to do:
And if he did not altogether – well,
Strauss is the next advance. All Strauss should be
I might be also. But to what result?
He looks upon no future: Luther did.                          580
What can I gain on the denying side?
Ice makes no conflagration. State the facts,
Read the text right, emancipate the world –
The emancipated world enjoys itself
With scarce a thank-you – Blougram told it first
It could not owe a farthing, not to him
More than St Paul! 'twould press its pay, you think?
Then add there's still that plaguey hundredth chance
Strauss may be wrong. And so a risk is run –
For what gain? not for Luther's, who secured           590
A real heaven in his heart throughout his life,
Supposing death a little altered things!

   'Ay, but since really I lack faith,' you cry,
'I run the same risk really on all sides,
In cool indifference as bold unbelief.
As well be Strauss as swing 'twixt Paul and him.
It's not worth having, such imperfect faith,
Nor more available to do faith's work
Than unbelief like yours. Whole faith, or none!'

   Softly, my friend! I must dispute that point.      600
Once own the use of faith, I'll find you faith.
We're back on Christian ground. You call for faith;
I show you doubt, to prove that faith exists.
The more of doubt, the stronger faith, I say,
If faith o'ercomes doubt. How I know it does?
By life and man's free will, God gave for that!

To mould life as we choose it, shows our choice:
That's our one act, the previous work's His own.
You criticise the soil? it reared this tree –
This broad life and whatever fruit it bears! 610
What matter though I doubt at every pore,
Head-doubts, heart-doubts, doubts at my fingers' ends.
Doubts in the trivial work of every day,
Doubts at the very bases of my soul
In the grand moments when she probes herself –
If finally I have a life to show,
The thing I did, brought out in evidence
Against the thing done to me underground
By Hell and all its brood, for ought I know?
I say, whence sprang this? Shows it faith or doubt? 620
All's doubt in me; where's break of faith in this?
It is the idea, the feeling and the love
God means mankind should strive for and show forth,
Whatever be the process to that end, –
And not historic knowledge, logic sound,
And metaphysical acumen, sure!
'What think ye of Christ,' friend? when all's done and said,
You like this Christianity or not?
It may be false, but will you wish it true?
Has it your vote to be so if it can? 630
Trust you an instinct silenced long ago
That will break silence and enjoin you love
What mortified philosophy is hoarse,
And all in vain, with bidding you despise?
If you desire faith – then you've faith enough.
What else seeks God – nay, what else seek ourselves?
You form a notion of me, we'll suppose,
On hearsay; it's a favourable one:
'But still' (you add), 'there was no such good man,
Because of contradictions in the facts. 640
One proves, for instance, he was born in Rome,
This Blougram – yet throughout the tales of him
I see he figures as an Englishman.'
Well, the two things are reconcileable.
But would I rather you discovered that

Subjoining – 'Still, what matter though they be?
Blougram – concerns me nought, born here or there.'

    Pure faith indeed – you know not what you ask!
Naked belief in God the Omnipotent,
Omniscient, Omnipresent, sears too much                          650
The sense of conscious creatures to be borne.
It were the seeing him, no flesh shall dare.
Some think, Creation's meant to show him forth:
I say, it's meant to hide him all it can,
And that's what all the blessed Evil's for.
It's use in time is to environ us,
Our breath, our drop of dew, with shield enough
Against that sight till we can bear its stress.
Under a vertical sun, the exposed brain
And lidless eye and disemprisoned heart                         660
Less certainly would wither up at once
Than mind, confronted with the truth of Him.
But time and earth case-harden us to live;
The feeblest sense is trusted most; the child
Feels God a moment, ichors o'er the place,
Plays on and grows to be a man like us.
With me, faith means perpetual unbelief
Kept quiet like the snake 'neath Michael's foot
Who stands calm just because he feels it writhe.
Or, if that's too ambitious, – here's my box –                  670
I need the excitation of a pinch
Threatening the torpor of the inside-nose
Nigh on the imminent sneeze that never comes.
'Leave it in peace' advise the simple folk –
Make it aware of peace by itching-fits,
Say I – let doubt occasion still more faith!

    You'll say, once all believed, man, woman, child,
In that dear middle-age these noodles praise.
How you'd exult if I could put you back
Six hundred years, blot out cosmogony,                          680
Geology, ethnology, what not,
(Greek endings, each the little passing-bell
That signifies some faith's about to die)
And set you square with Genesis again, –

When such a traveller told you his last news,
He saw the ark a-top of Ararat
But did not climb there since 'twas getting dusk
And robber-bands infest the mountain's foot!
How should you feel, I ask, in such an age,
How act? As other people felt and did;                          690
With soul more blank than this decanter's knob,
Believe – and yet lie, kill, rob, fornicate
Full in belief's face, like the beast you'd be!

No, when the fight begins within himself,
A man's worth something. God stoops o'er his head,
Satan looks up between his feet – both tug –
He's left, himself, in the middle: the soul wakes
And grows. Prolong that battle through his life!
Never leave growing till the life to come!
Here, we've got callous to the Virgin's winks            700
That used to puzzle people wholesomely –
Men have outgrown the shame of being fools.
What are the laws of Nature, not to bend
If the Church bid them, brother Newman asks.
Up with the Immaculate Conception, then –
On to the rack with faith – is my advice!
Will not that hurry us upon our knees
Knocking our breasts, 'It can't be – yet it shall!
Who am I, the worm, to argue with my Pope?
Low things confound the high things!' and so forth.     710
That's better than acquitting God with grace
As some folks do. He's tried – no case is proved,
Philosophy is lenient – He may go!

You'll say – the old system's not so obsolete
But men believe still: ay, but who and where?
King Bomba's lazzaroni foster yet
The sacred flame, so Antonelli writes;
But even of these, what ragamuffin-saint
Believes God watches him continually,
As he believes in fire that it will burn,                        720
Or rain that it will drench him? Break fire's law,
Sin against rain, although the penalty

Be just singe or soaking? No, he smiles;
Those laws are laws that can enforce themselves.

    The sum of all is – yes, my doubt is great,
My faith's the greater – then my faith's enough.
I have read much, thought much, experienced much,
Yet would die rather than avow my fear
The Naples' liquefaction may be false,
When set to happen by the palace-clock                          730
According to the clouds or dinner-time.
I hear you recommend, I might at least
Eliminate, decrassify my faith
Since I adopt it; keeping what I must
And leaving what I can – such points as this!
I won't – this is, I can't throw one away.
Supposing there's no truth in what I said
About the need of trials to man's faith,
Still, when you bid me purify the same,
To such a process I discern no end,                             740
Clearing off one excrescence to see two;
There's ever a next in size, now grown as big,
That meets the knife – I cut and cut again!
First cut the Liquefaction, what comes last
But Fichte's clever cut at God himself?
Experimentalize on sacred things?
I trust nor hand nor eye nor heart nor brain
To stop betimes: they all get drunk alike.
The first step, I am master not to take.

    You'd find the cutting-process to your taste              750
As much as leaving growths of lies unpruned,
Nor see more danger in it, you retort.
Your taste's worth mine; but my taste proves more wise
When we consider that the steadfast hold
On the extreme end of the chain of faith
Gives all the advantage, makes the difference,
With the rough purblind mass we seek to rule.
We are their lords, or they are free of us
Just as we tighten or relax that hold.
So, other matters equal, we'll revert                          760

To the first problem – which if solved my way
And thrown into the balance turns the scale –
How we may lead a comfortable life,
How suit our luggage to the cabin's size.

Of course you are remarking all this time
How narrowly and grossly I view life,
Respect the creature-comforts, care to rule
The masses, and regard complacently
'The cabin,' in our old phrase! Well, I do.
I act for, talk for, live for this world now,                    770
As this world calls for action, life and talk –
No prejudice to what next world may prove,
Whose new laws and requirements my best pledge
To observe them, is that I observe these now,
Doing hereafter what I do meanwhile.
Let us concede (gratuitously though)
Next life relieves the soul of body, yields
Pure spiritual enjoyments: well, my friend,
Why lose this life in the meantime, since its use
May be to make the next life more intense?                    780

Do you know, I have often had a dream
(Work it up in your next month's article)
Of man's poor spirit in its progress still
Losing true life for ever and a day
Through ever trying to be and ever being
In the evolution of successive spheres,
Before its actual sphere and place of life,
Halfway into the next, which having reached,
It shoots with corresponding foolery
Halfway into the next still, on and off!                    790
As when a traveller, bound from north to south,
Scouts fur in Russia – what's its use in France?
In France spurns flannel – where's its need in Spain?
In Spain drops cloth – too cumbrous for Algiers!
Linen goes next, and last the skin itself
A superfluity at Timbuctoo.
When, through his journey, was the fool at ease?
I'm at ease now, friend – worldly in this world

I take and like its way of life; I think
My brothers who administer the means                    800
Live better for my comfort – that's good too;
And God, if he pronounce upon it all,
Approves my service, which is better still.
If He keeps silence, – why for you or me
Or that brute-beast pulled-up in to-day's 'Times,'
What odds is't, save to ourselves, what life we lead?

    You meet me at this issue – you declare,
All special pleading done with, truth is truth,
And justifies itself by undreamed ways.
You don't fear but it's better, if we doubt,               810
To say so, acting up to our truth perceived
However feebly. Do then, – act away!
'Tis there I'm on the watch for you! How one acts
Is, both of us agree, our chief concern:
And how you'll act is what I fain would see
If, like the candid person you appear,
You dare to make the most of your life's scheme
As I of mine, live up to its full law
Since there's no higher law that counterchecks.
Put natural religion to the test                           820
You've just demolished the revealed with – quick,
Down to the root of all that checks your will,
All prohibition to lie, kill, and thieve
Or even to be an atheistic priest!
Suppose a pricking to incontinence –
Philosophers deduce you chastity
Or shame, from just the fact that at the first
Whoso embraced a woman in the plain,
Threw club down, and forewent his brains beside,
So stood a ready victim in the reach                       830
Of any brother-savage club in hand –
Hence saw the use of going out of sight
In wood or cave to prosecute his loves –
I read this in a French book t'other day.
Does law so analyzed coerce you much?
Oh, men spin clouds of fuzz where matters end,
But you who reach where the first thread begins,

You'll soon cut that! – which means you can, but won't
Through certain instincts, blind, unreasoned-out,
You dare not set aside, you can't tell why,                    840
But there they are, and so you let them rule.
Then, friend, you seem as much a slave as I,
A liar, conscious coward and hypocrite,
Without the good the slave expects to get,
Suppose he has a master after all!
You own your instincts – why what else do I,
Who want, am made for, and must have a God
Ere I can be ought, do ought? – no mere name
Want, but the true thing with what proves its truth,
To wit, a relation from that thing to me,                    850
Touching from head to foot – which touch I feel,
And with it take the test, this life of ours!
I live my life here; yours you dare not live.

Not as I state it, who (you please subjoin)
Disfigure such a life and call it names,
While, in your mind, remains another way
For simple men: knowledge and power have rights,
But ignorance and weakness have rights too.
There needs no crucial effort to find truth
If here or there or anywhere about –                    860
We ought to turn each side, try hard and see,
And if we can't, be glad we've earned at least
The right, by one laborious proof the more,
To graze in peace earth's pleasant pasturage.
Men are not gods, but, properly, are brutes.
Something we may see, all we cannot see –
What need of lying? I say, I see all,
And swear to each detail the most minute,
In what I think a man's face – you, mere cloud:
I swear I hear him speak and see him wink,                    870
For fear, if once I drop the emphasis,
Mankind may doubt if there's a cloud at all.
You take the simpler life – ready to see,
Willing to see – for no cloud's worth a face –
And leaving quiet what no strength can move,
And which, who bids you move? who has the right?

I bid you; but you are God's sheep, not mine –
'*Pastor est tui Dominus.*' You find
In these the pleasant pastures of this life
Much you may eat without the least offence,     880
Much you don't eat because your maw objects,
Much you would eat but that your fellow-flock
Open great eyes at you and even butt,
And thereupon you like your friends so much
You cannot please yourself, offending them –
Though when they seem exorbitantly sheep,
You weigh your pleasure with their butts and kicks
And strike the balance. Sometimes certain fears
Restrain you – real checks since you find them so –
Sometimes you please yourself and nothing checks;   890
And thus you graze through life with not one lie,
And like it best.

                But do you, in truth's name?
If so, you beat – which means – you are not I –
Who needs must make earth mine and feed my fill
Not simply unbutted at, unbickered with,
But motioned to the velvet of the sward
By those obsequious wethers' very selves.
Look at me, sir; my age is double yours.
At yours, I knew beforehand, so enjoyed,
What now I should be – as, permit the word,    900
I pretty well imagine your whole range
And stretch of tether twenty years to come.
We both have minds and bodies much alike.
In truth's name, don't you want my bishopric,
My daily bread, my influence and my state?
You're young, I'm old, you must be old one day;
Will you find then, as I do hour by hour,
Women their lovers kneel to, that cut curls
From your fat lap-dog's ears to grace a brooch –
Dukes, that petition just to kiss your ring –    910
With much beside you know or may conceive?
Suppose we die to-night: well, here am I,
Such were my gains, life bore this fruit to me,
While writing all the same my articles

On music, poetry, the fictile vase
Found at Albano, or Anacreon's Greek.
But you – the highest honour in your life,
The thing you'll crown yourself with, all your days,
Is – dining here and drinking this last glass
I pour you out in sign of amity                                      920
Before we part for ever. Of your power
And social influence, worldly worth in short,
Judge what's my estimation by the fact –
I do not condescend to enjoin, beseech,
Hint secrecy on one of all these words!
You're shrewd and know that should you publish it
The world would brand the lie – my enemies first,
'Who'd sneer – the bishop's an arch-hypocrite,
And knave perhaps, but not so frank a fool,'
Whereas I should not dare for both my ears                           930
Breathe one such syllable, smile one such smile,
Before my chaplain who reflects myself –
My shade's so much more potent than your flesh.
What's your reward, self-abnegating friend?
Stood you confessed of those exceptional
And privileged great natures that dwarf mine –
A zealot with a mad ideal in reach,
A poet just about to print his ode,
A statesman with a scheme to stop this war,
An artist whose religion is his art,                                 940
I should have nothing to object! such men
Carry the fire, all things grow warm to them,
Their drugget's worth my purple, they beat me.
But you, – you're just as little those as I –
You, Gigadibs, who, thirty years of age,
Write statedly for Blackwood's Magazine,
Believe you see two points in Hamlet's soul
Unseized by the Germans yet – which view you'll print –
Meantime the best you have to show being still
That lively lightsome article we took                                950
Almost for the true Dickens, – what's the name?
'The Slum and Cellar – or Whitechapel life
Limned after dark!' it made me laugh, I know,
And pleased a month and brought you in ten pounds.

– Success I recognise and compliment,
And therefore give you, if you please, three words
(The card and pencil-scratch is quite enough)
Which whether here, in Dublin, or New York,
Will get you, prompt as at my eyebrow's wink,
Such terms as never you aspired to get                           960
In all our own reviews and some not ours.
Go write your lively sketches – be the first
'Blougram, or The Eccentric Confidence' –
Or better simply say, 'The Outward-bound.'
Why, men as soon would throw it in my teeth
As copy and quote the infamy chalked broad
About me on the church-door opposite.
You will not wait for that experience though,
I fancy, howsoever you decide,
To discontinue – not detesting, not                              970
Defaming, but at least – despising me!

————

Over his wine so smiled and talked his hour
Sylvester Blougram, styled *in partibus*
*Episcopus, nec non* – (the deuce knows what
It's changed to by our novel hierarchy)
With Gigadibs the literary man,
Who played with spoons, explored his plate's design,
And ranged the olive stones about its edge,
While the great bishop rolled him out of his mind.

  For Blougram, he believed, say, half he spoke.          980
The other portion, as he shaped it thus
For argumentatory purposes,
He felt his foe was foolish to dispute.
Some arbitrary accidental thoughts
That crossed his mind, amusing because new,
He chose to represent as fixtures there,
Invariable convictions (such they seemed
Beside his interlocutor's loose cards
Flung daily down, and not the same way twice)
While certain hell-deep instincts, man's weak tongue     990

Is never bold to utter in their truth
Because styled hell-deep ('tis an old mistake
To place hell at the bottom of the earth)
He ignored these, – not having in readiness
Their nomenclature and philosophy:
He said true things, but called them by wrong names.
'On the whole,' he thought, 'I justify myself
On every point where cavillers like this
Oppugn my life: he tries one kind of fence –
I close – he's worsted, that's enough for him;          1000
He's on the ground! if the ground should break away
I take my stand on, there's a firmer yet
Beneath it, both of us may sink and reach.
His ground was over mine and broke the first.
So let him sit with me this many a year!'

He did not sit five minutes. Just a week
Sufficed his sudden healthy vehemence.
(Something had stuck him in the 'Outward-bound'
Another way than Blougram's purpose was)
And having bought, not cabin-furniture                  1010
But settler's-implements (enough for three)
And started for Australia – there, I hope,
By this time he has tested his first plough,
And studied his last chapter of St John.

# Holy-Cross Day

## On Which the Jews were Forced
## to Attend an Annual Christian Sermon in Rome

['Now was come about Holy-Cross Day, and now must my lord
preach his first sermon to the Jews: as it was of old cared for in
the merciful bowels of the Church, that, so to speak, a crumb at
least from her conspicuous table here in Rome should be, though
but once yearly, cast to the famishing dogs, under-trampled and
bespitten-upon beneath the feet of the guests. And a moving sight
in truth, this, of so many of the besotted blind restif and ready-to-
perish Hebrews! now maternally brought – nay (for He saith,
'Compel them to come in') haled, as it were, by the head and
hair, and against their obstinate hearts, to partake of the
heavenly grace. What awakening, what striving with tears, what
working of a yeasty conscience! Nor was my lord wanting to
himself on so apt an occasion; witness the abundance of
conversions which did incontinently reward him: though not to
my lord be altogether the glory' – *Diary by the Bishop's Secretary*,
1600]

Though what the Jews really said, on thus being driven to
church, was rather to this effect:

1

Fee, faw, fum! bubble and squeak!
Blessedest Thursday's the fat of the week.
Rumble and tumble, sleek and rough,
Stinking and savoury, smug and gruff,
Take the church-road, for the bell's due chime
Gives us the summons – 'tis sermon-time!

2

Boh, here's Barnabas! Job, that's you?
Up stumps Solomon – bustling too?
Shame, man! greedy beyond your years

To handsel the bishop's shaving-shears?                    10
Fair play's a jewel! Leave friends in the lurch?
Stand on a line ere you start for the church!


### 3

Higgledy piggledy, packed we lie,
Rats in a hamper, swine in a stye,
Wasps in a bottle, frogs in a sieve,
Worms in a carcase, fleas in a sleeve.
Hist! square shoulders, settle your thumbs
And buzz for the bishop – here he comes.


### 4

Bow, wow, wow – a bone for the dog!
I liken his Grace to an acorned hog.                       20
What, a boy at his side, with the bloom of a lass,
To help and handle my lord's hour-glass!
Didst ever behold so lithe a chine?
His cheek hath laps like a fresh-singed swine.


### 5

Aaron's asleep – shove hip to haunch,
Or somebody deal him a dig in the paunch!
Look at the purse with the tassel and knob,
And the gown with the angel and thingumbob!
What's he at, quotha? reading his text!
Now you've his curtsey – and what comes next        30


### 6

See to our converts – you doomed black dozen –
No stealing away – nor cog nor cozen!
You five, that were thieves, deserve it fairly;
You seven, that were beggars, will live less sparely;
You took your turn and dipped in the hat,
Got fortune – and fortune gets you; mind that!


### 7

Give your first groan – compunction's at work;
And soft! from a Jew you mount to a Turk.
Lo, Micah, – the selfsame beard on chin

He was four times already converted in!      40
Here's a knife, clip quick – it's a sign of grace –
Or he ruins us all with his hanging-face.

### 8

Whom now is the bishop a-leering at?
I know a point where his text falls pat.
I'll tell him to-morrow, a word just now
Went to my heart and made me vow
I meddle no more with the worst of trades –
Let somebody else pay his serenades.

### 9

Groan all together now, whee – hee – hee!
It's a-work, it's a-work, ah, woe is me!      50
It began, when a herd of us, picked and placed,
Were spurred through the Corso, stripped to the waist;
Jew brutes, with sweat and blood well spent
To usher in worthily Christian Lent.

### 10

It grew, when the hangman entered our bounds,
Yelled, pricked us out to his church like hounds:
It got to a pitch, when the hand indeed
Which gutted my purse would throttle my creed:
And it overflows when, to even the odd,
Men I helped to their sins help me to their God.      60

### 11

But now, while the scapegoats leave our flock,
And the rest sit silent and count the clock,
Since forced to muse the appointed time
On these precious facts and truths sublime, –
Let us fitly employ it, under our breath,
In saying Ben Ezra's Song of Death.

### 12

For Rabbi Ben Ezra, the night he died,
Called sons and sons' sons to his side,
And spoke, 'This world has been harsh and strange;

Something is wrong: there needeth a change.          70
But what, or where? at the last or first?
In one point only we sinned, at worst.


### 13

The Lord will have mercy on Jacob yet,
And again in his brother see Israel set.
When Judah beholds Jerusalem,
The stranger-seed shall be joined to them:
To Jacob's House shall the Gentiles cleave.
So the Prophet saith and his sons believe.


### 14

Ay, the children of the chosen race
Shall carry and bring them to their place:          80
In the land of the Lord shall lead the same,
Bondsmen and handmaids. Who shall blame,
When the slaves enslave, the oppressed ones o'er
The oppressor triumph for evermore?


### 15

God spoke, and gave us the word to keep
Bade never fold the hands nor sleep
'Mid a faithless world, – at watch and ward,
Till Christ at the end relieve our guard.
By His servant Moses the watch was set:
Though near upon cock-crow, we keep it yet.         90


### 16

Thou! if thou wast He, who at mid-watch came,
By the starlight, naming a dubious name!
And if, too heavy with sleep – too rash
With fear – O Thou, if that martyr-gash
Fell on Thee coming to take thine own,
And we gave the Cross, when we owed the Throne –


### 17

Thou art the Judge. We are bruised thus.
But, the Judgment over, join sides with us!
Thine too is the cause! and not more thine

Than ours, is the work of these dogs and swine,          100
Whose life laughs through and spits at their creed!
Who maintain Thee in word, and defy Thee in deed!


### 18

We withstood Christ then? Be mindful how
At least we withstand Barabbas now!
Was our outrage sore? But the worst we spared,
To have called these – Christians, – had we dared!
Let defiance to them pay mistrust of Thee,
And Rome make amends for Calvary!


### 19

By the torture, prolonged from age to age,
By the infamy, Israel's heritage,                        110
By the Ghetto's plague, by the garb's disgrace,
By the badge of shame, by the felon's place,
By the branding-tool, the bloody whip,
And the summons to Christian fellowship, –


### 20

We boast our proof that at least the Jew
Would wrest Christ's name from the Devil's crew.
Thy face took never so deep a shade
But we fought them in it, God our aid!
A trophy to bear, as we march, thy band,
South, East, and on to the Pleasant Land!'          120


[The present Pope abolished this bad business of the
Sermon – R. B.]

# Two in the Campagna

### 1

I wonder do you feel to-day
    As I have felt since, hand in hand,
We sat down on the grass, to stray
    In spirit better through the land,
This morn of Rome and May?

### 2

For me, I touched a thought, I know,
    Has tantalized me many times,
(Like turns of thread the spiders throw
    Mocking across our path) for rhymes
To catch at and let go                                      10

### 3

Help me to hold it! First it left
    The yellowing fennel, run to seed
There, branching from the brickwork's cleft,
    Some old tomb's ruin: yonder weed
Took up the floating weft,

### 4

Where one small orange cup amassed
    Five beetles, – blind and green they grope
Among the honey-meal: and last,
    Everywhere on the grassy slope
I traced it. Hold it fast!                                  20

### 5

The champaign with its endless fleece
    Of feathery grasses everywhere!
Silence and passion, joy and peace,

An everlasting wash of air –
Rome's ghost since her decease.

### 6

Such life here, through such lengths of hours,
   Such miracles performed in play,
Such primal naked forms of flowers,
   Such letting nature have her way
While heaven looks from its towers!           30

### 7

How say you? Let us, O my dove,
   Let us be unashamed of soul,
As earth lies bare to heaven above!
   How is it under our control
To love or not to love?

### 8

I would that you were all to me,
   You that are just so much, no more.
Nor yours nor mine, nor slave nor free!
   Where does the fault lie? What the core
O' the wound, since wound must be?         40

### 9

I would I could adopt your will,
   See with your eyes, and set my heart
Beating by yours, and drink my fill
   At your soul's springs, – your part my part
In life, for good and ill.

### 10

No. I yearn upward, touch you close,
   Then stand away. I kiss your cheek,
Catch your soul's warmth, – I pluck the rose
   And love it more than tongue can speak –
Then the good minute goes.         50

### 11

Already how am I so far
   Out of that minute? Must I go

Still like the thistle-ball, no bar,
   Onward, whenever light winds blow
Fixed by no friendly star?

12

Just when I seemed about to learn!
   Where is the thread now? Off again!
The old trick! Only I discern —
   Infinite passion, and the pain
Of finite hearts that yearn.                    60

# Caliban upon Setebos; or Natural Theology in the Island

'Thou thoughtest that I was altogether such a one as thyself.'

['Will sprawl, now that the heat of day is best,
Flat on his belly in the pit's much mire,
With elbows wide, fists clenched to prop his chin.
And, while he kicks both feet in the cool slush,
And feels about his spine small eft-things course,
Run in and out each arm, and make him laugh:
And while above his head a pompion-plant,
Coating the cave-top as a brow its eye,
Creeps down to touch and tickle hair and beard,
And now a flower drops with a bee inside,                          10
And now a fruit to snap at, catch and crunch, –
He looks out o'er yon sea which sunbeams cross
And recross till they weave a spider-web
(Meshes of fire, some great fish breaks at times)
And talks to his own self, howe'er he please,
Touching that other, whom his dam called God.
Because to talk about Him, vexes – ha,
Could He but know! and time to vex is now,
When talk is safer than in winter-time.
Moreover Prosper and Miranda sleep                                20
In confidence he drudges at their task,
And it is good to cheat the pair, and gibe,
Letting the rank tongue blossom into speech.]

Setebos, Setebos, and Setebos!
'Thinketh, He dwelleth i' the cold o' the moon.

'Thinketh He made it, with the sun to match,
But not the stars; the stars came otherwise;
Only made clouds, winds, meteors, such as that:

Also this isle, what lives and grows thereon,
And snaky sea which rounds and ends the same.                    30

'Thinketh, it came of being ill at ease:
He hated that He cannot change His cold,
Nor cure its ache. 'Hath spied an icy fish
That longed to 'scape the rock-stream where she lived,
And thaw herself within the lukewarm brine
O' the lazy sea her stream thrusts far amid,
A crystal spike 'twixt two warm walls of wave;
Only, she ever sickened, found repulse
At the other kind of water, not her life,
(Green-dense and dim-delicious, bred o' the sun)                40
Flounced back from bliss she was not born to breathe,
And in her old bounds buried her despair,
Hating and loving warmth alike: so He.

'Thinketh, He made thereat the sun, this isle,
Trees and the fowls here, beast and creeping thing.
Yon otter, sleek-wet, black, lithe as a leech;
Yon auk, one fire-eye in a ball of foam,
That floats and feeds; a certain badger brown
He hath watched hunt with that slant white-wedge eye
By moonlight; and the pie with the long tongue                  50
That pricks deep into oakwarts for a worm,
And says a plain word when she finds her prize,
But will not eat the ants; the ants themselves
That build a wall of seeds and settled stalks
About their hole – He made all these and more,
Made all we see, and us, in spite: how else?
He could not, Himself, make a second self
To be His mate: as well have made Himself:
He would not make what he mislikes or slights,
An eyesore to Him, or not worth His pains:                      60
But did, in envy, listlessness or sport,
Make what Himself would fain, in a manner, be –
Weaker in most points, stronger in a few,
Worthy, and yet mere playthings all the while,
Things He admires and mocks too, – that is it.
Because, so brave, so better though they be,

It nothing skills if He begin to plague.
Look now, I melt a gourd-fruit into mash,
Add honeycomb and pods, I have perceived,
Which bite like finches when they bill and kiss, –         70
Then, when froth rises bladdery, drink up all,
Quick, quick, till maggots scamper through my brain;
Last, throw me on my back i' the seeded thyme,
And wanton, wishing I were born a bird.
Put case, unable to be what I wish,
I yet could make a live bird out of clay:
Would not I take clay, pinch my Caliban
Able to fly? – for, there, see, he hath wings,
And great comb like the hoopoe's to admire,
And there, a sting to do his foes offence,                 80
There, and I will that he begin to live,
Fly to yon rock-top, nip me off the horns
Of grigs high up that make the merry din,
Saucy through their veined wings, and mind me not.
In which feat, if his leg snapped, brittle clay,
And he lay stupid-like, – why, I should laugh;
And if he, spying me, should fall to weep,
Beseech me to be good, repair his wrong,
Bid his poor leg smart less or grow again, –
Well, as the chance were, this might take or else          90
Not take my fancy: I might hear his cry,
And give the mankin three sound legs for one,
Or pluck the other off, leave him like an egg,
And lessoned he was mine and merely clay.
Were this no pleasure, lying in the thyme,
Drinking the mash, with brain become alive,
Making and marring clay at will? So He.

'Thinketh, such shows nor right nor wrong in Him,
Nor kind, nor cruel: He is strong and Lord.
'Am strong myself compared to yonder crabs                 100
That march now from the mountain to the sea;
'Let twenty pass, and stone the twenty-first,
Loving not, hating not, just choosing so.
'Say, the first straggler that boasts purple spots
Shall join the file, one pincer twisted off;

'Say, this bruised fellow shall receive a worm,
And two worms he whose nippers end in red;
As it likes me each time, I do: so He.

Well then, 'supposeth He is good i' the main,
Placable if His mind and ways were guessed,                      110
But rougher than His handiwork, be sure!
Oh, He hath made things worthier than Himself,
And envieth that, so helped, such things do more
Than He who made them! What consoles but this?
That they, unless through Him, do naught at all,
And must submit: what other use in things?
'Hath cut a pipe of pithless elder joint
That, blown through, gives exact the scream o' the jay
When from her wing you twitch the feathers blue:
Sound this, and little birds that hate the jay                    120
Flock within stone's throw, glad their foe is hurt:
Put case such pipe could prattle and boast forsooth
'I catch the birds, I am the crafty thing,
'I make the cry my maker cannot make
'With his great round mouth; he must blow through mine!'
Would not I smash it with my foot? So He.

But wherefore rough, why cold and ill at ease?
Aha, that is a question! Ask, for that,
What knows, – the something over Setebos
That made Him, or He, may be, found and fought,                   130
Worsted, drove off and did to nothing, perchance.
There may be something quiet o'er His head,
Out of His reach, that feels nor joy nor grief,
Since both derive from weakness in some way.
I joy because the quails come; would not joy
Could I bring quails here when I have a mind:
This Quiet, all it hath a mind to, doth.
'Esteemeth stars the outposts of its couch,
But never spends much thought nor care that way.
It may look up, work up, – the worse for those                    140
It works on! 'Careth but for Setebos
The many-handed as a cuttle-fish,
Who, making Himself feared through what He does,

Looks up, first, and perceives he cannot soar
To what is quiet and hath happy life;
Next looks down here, and out of very spite
Makes this a bauble-world to ape yon real,
These good things to match those as hips do grapes.
'Tis solace making baubles, ay, and sport.
Himself peeped late, eyed Prosper at his books          150
Careless and lofty, lord now of the isle:
Vexed, 'stitched a book of broad leaves, arrow-shaped,
Wrote thereon, he knows what, prodigious words;
Has peeled a wand and called it by a name;
Weareth at whiles for an enchanter's robe
The eyed skin of a supple oncelot;
And hath an ounce sleeker than youngling mole,
A four-legged serpent he makes cower and couch,
Now snarl, now hold its breath and mind his eye,
And saith she is Miranda and my wife:          160
'Keeps for his Ariel a tall pouch-bill crane
He bids go wade for fish and straight disgorge;
Also a sea-beast, lumpish, which he snared,
Blinded the eyes of, and brought somewhat tame,
And split its toe-webs, and now pens the drudge
In a hole o' the rock and calls him Caliban;
A bitter heart that bides its time and bites.
'Plays thus at being Prosper in a way,
Taketh his mirth with make-believes: so He.

His dam held that the Quiet made all things          170
Which Setebos vexed only: 'holds not so.
Who made them weak, meant weakness He might vex.
Had He meant other, while His hand was in,
Why not make horny eyes no thorn could prick,
Or plate my scalp with bone against the snow,
Or overscale my flesh 'neath joint and joint,
Like an orc's armour? Ay, – so spoil His sport!
He is the One now: only He doth all.

'Saith, He may like, perchance, what profits Him.
Ay, himself loves what does him good; but why?          180
'Gets good no otherwise. This blinded beast

Loves whoso places flesh-meat on his nose,
But, had he eyes, would want to help, but hate
Or love, just as it liked him: He hath eyes.
Also it pleaseth Setebos to work,
Use all His hands, and exercise much craft,
By no means for the love of what is worked.
'Tasteth, himself, no finer good i' the world
When all goes right, in this safe summer-time,
And he wants little, hungers, aches not much,                    190
Than trying what to do with wit and strength.
'Falls to make something: 'piled yon pile of turfs,
And squared and stuck there squares of soft white chalk,
And, with a fish-tooth, scratched a moon on each,
And set up endwise certain spikes of tree,
And crowned the whole with a sloth's skull a-top,
Found dead i' the woods, too hard for one to kill.
No use at all i' the work, the work's sole sake;
'Shall some day knock it down again: so He.

'Saith He is terrible: watch His feats in proof!                  200
One hurricane will spoil six good months' hope.
He hath a spite against me, that I know,
Just as He favours Prosper, who knows why?
So it is, all the same, as well I find.
'Wove wattles half the winter, fenced them firm
With stone and stake to stop she-tortoises
Crawling to lay their eggs here: well, one wave,
Feeling the foot of Him upon its neck,
Gaped as a snake does, lolled out its large tongue,
And licked the whole labour flat: so much for spite.             210
'Saw a ball flame down late (yonder it lies)
Where, half an hour before, I slept i' the shade:
Often they scatter sparkles: there is force!
'Dug up a newt He may have envied once
And turned to stone, shut up inside a stone.
Please Him and hinder this? – What Prosper does?
Aha, if He would tell me how! Not He!
There is the sport: discover how or die!
All need not die, for of the things o' the isle
Some flee afar, some dive, some run up trees;                    220

Those at His mercy, – why, they please Him most
When . . . when . . . well, never try the same way twice!
Repeat what act has pleased, He may grow wroth.
You must not know His ways, and play Him off,
Sure of the issue. 'Doth the like himself:
'Spareth a squirrel that it nothing fears
But steals the nut from underneath my thumb,
And when I threat, bites stoutly in defence:
'Spareth an urchin that contrariwise,
Curls up into a ball, pretending death                          230
For fright at my approach: the two ways please.
But what would move my choler more than this,
That either creature counted on its life
To-morrow and next day and all days to come,
Saying, forsooth, in the inmost of its heart,
'Because he did so yesterday with me,
'And otherwise with such another brute,
'So must he do henceforth and always.' – Ay?
Would teach the reasoning couple what 'must' means!
'Doth as he likes, or wherefore Lord? So He.          240

'Conceiveth all things will continue thus,
And we shall have to live in fear of Him
So long as He lives, keeps His strength: no change,
If He have done His best, make no new world
To please Him more, so leave off watching this, –
If He surprise not even the Quiet's self
Some strange day, – or, suppose, grow into it
As grubs grow butterflies: else, here are we,
And there is He, and nowhere help at all.

'Believeth with the life, the pain shall stop.          250
His dam held different, that after death
He both plagued enemies and feasted friends:
Idly! He doth His worst in this our life,
Giving just respite lest we die through pain,
Saving last pain for worst, – with which, an end.
Meanwhile, the best way to escape His ire,
Is, not to seem too happy. 'Sees, himself,
Yonder two flies, with purple films and pink,

Bask on the pompion-bell above; kills both.
'Sees two black painful beetles roll their ball                                        260
On head and tail as if to save their lives:
Moves them the stick away they strive to clear.

Even so, 'would have Him misconceive, suppose
This Caliban strives hard and ails no less,
And always, above all else, envies Him;
Wherefore he mainly dances on dark nights,
Moans in the sun, gets under holes to laugh,
And never speaks his mind save housed as now:
Outside, 'groans, curses. If He caught me here,
O'erheard this speech, and asked. 'What chucklest at?'                              270
'Would, to appease Him, cut a finger off,
Or of my three kid yearlings burn the best,
Or let the toothsome apples rot on tree,
Or push my tame beast for the orc to taste:
While myself lit a fire, and made a song
And sung it, *What I hate, be consecrate*
*'To celebrate Thee and Thy state, no mate*
*'For Thee; what see for envy in poor me?'*
Hoping the while, since evils sometimes mend,
Warts rub away and sores are cured with slime,                                      280
That some strange day, will either the Quiet catch
And conquer Setebos, or likelier He
Decrepit may doze, doze, as good as die.
[What, what? A curtain o'er the world at once!
Crickets stop hissing; not a bird – or, yes,
There scuds His raven that has told Him all!
It was fool's play, this prattling! Ha! The wind
Shoulders the pillared dust, death's house o' the move,
And fast invading fires begin! White blaze –
A tree's head snaps – and there, there, there, there, there,                        290
His thunder follows! Fool to gibe at Him!
Lo! 'Lieth flat and loveth Setebos!
'Maketh his teeth meet through his upper lip,
Will let those quails fly, will not eat this month
One little mess of whelks, so he may 'scape!]

# Notes

**p. 3 *My Last Duchess*:** First published in *Dramatic Lyrics*. Probably modelled on Alfonso II, fifth Duke of Ferrara (b. 1533); if so, the Duchess was Lucrezia de Medici. After her death (poisoning was suspected at the time) Ferrara married a noblewoman from Innsbruck. **3 Frà Pandolf** and **56 Claus of Innsbruck:** both fictional artists.

**p. 5 *Soliloquy of the Spanish Cloister*:** First published in *Dramatic Lyrics* (1842) under a different title. **10 Salve tibi:** 'Hail to thee!' (Latin). **16 Swine's Snout:** dandelion. **31 Barbary corsair's:** Barbary on the north African coast, was associated with pirates. **39 Arian:** a follower of Arius and therefore heretical. **49 Galatians:** Browning's error here, since no such text exists. **56 Manichee:** referring to another heretical sect. **60 Belial's gripe:** the grip of the Devil. **70 Hy, Zy, Hine:** generally thought to be either nonsense words or onomatopoeia. **71–2 Plena gratiâ/Ave, Virgo:** 'Full of grace, hail, virgin' (Latin – a slightly altered version of the standard invocation).

**p. 8 *Johannes Agricola in Meditation*:** In *Dramatic Lyrics* this and the next poem were coupled under the heading 'Madhouse Cells, I and II'. The speaker is Johannes Schnitter or Schneider (1494–1566), who adopted the name Agricola, and was a founder of Antinomian doctrine, based on predestination. Browning was hostile to the Antinomian notion of an elect group of Christians predetermined to be saved and therefore above moral law.

**p. 12 *The Pied Piper of Hamelin*:** First published in *Dramatic Lyrics*. W.M. is William Macready, who was ill at the time of the writing of the poem. **89 Tartary:** on the Caspian Sea (Cham is the name of the ruler [Khan]). **91 Nizam:** eighth-century ruler of Hyderabad. **136 psaltery:** stringed instrument. **138 puncheon:** cask. **177 Bagdat:** Baghdad. **179 Caliph:** Muslim ruler. **258 ff:** see Matthew xix.24.

**p. 23 *The Bishop Orders His Tomb at Saint Praxed's Church*:** First collected in *Dramatic Romances and Lyrics*. The church of Santa Prassede is near Rome. **1**: see Ecclesiastes i.2. **31 onion-stone:** inferior marble which tends to peel. **41 olive-frail:** basket. **46 Frascati:** town near Rome. **54 antique-black:** nero antica, a costly black stone. **57 Pans and Nymphs:** both have licentious connotations. **58 tripod, thyrsus:** three-legged stool often associated with Dionysus and thus revelry. **77 Tully:** Marcus Tullius Cicero (106–43 BC), Roman rhetorician. **79 Ulpian:** Domintius Ulpianus (AD 170–228), a writer of Latin inferior to Cicero's. **89 mortcloth:** funeral pall. **99 ELUSCEBAT:** 'He was illustrious'; in Ulpian's style rather than Cicero's, which would have been 'elucebat'. **108 vizor and a Term:** a mask and a bust.

**p. 29 *Fra Lippo Lippi*:** First published in *Men and Women*. Browning's main souce for Lippo Lippi's life was Vasari's *Lives of the Artists*. **7 Carmine:** Carmelite monastery in Florence. **17 Cosimo de Medici:** banker and patron of the arts who also had power in Florence. **34 John Baptist's head a-dangle:** according to Vasari this was the subject of a painting by Lippo. **53 *Flower o' the broom*:** Tuscan folk song. **73 St Jerome:** appears in one of Lippo's paintings. **88 Aunt Lapaccia:** biographical detail from Vasari. **121 Eight:** Florentine magistrates. **130 antiphonary:** book of choral music. **139 Camaldolese:** religious order founded near Florence in 1027. **140 Preaching Friars:** Dominicans. **189 Giotto:** Giotto di Bondone (c. 1267–1337), painter and architect. **196 Herodias:** mother of Salome who dances before Herod and asks for John the Baptist's head; Browning here repeats an error in Vasari. **235 Angelico:** Fra Angelico (1387–1455), painter. **236 Lorenzo:** Lorenzo Monaco (c. 1370–1425), painter and Fra Angelico's master. **276 Guidi:** Tomaso Guidi (1401–28?). He was Lippo's teacher, not his pupil; Browning's error here. **307 cullion:** rascal **323 St Laurence:** saint who was roasted alive (AD 258). **324 Prato:** town near Florence. **328 Deacon:** i.e. Laurence. **346 Sant' Ambrogio's:** convent in Florence. The painting referred to is Lippo's *Coronation of the Virgin*. **354 Saint John:** patron saint of Florentines. **355 Saint Ambrose:** Lippo confuses the patron saint of Sant' Ambrogio with Ambrose the Camaldulian (1386–1439). **377 *Iste perfecit opus!*:** 'This man accomplished/arranged the work'. **381 hot cockles:** a country game; here used as a euphemism for sexual activity. **387 Saint Lucy:** a virgin martyr.

**p. 39 *A Toccata of Galuppi's*:** First published in *Men and Women*. Baldassare Galuppi (1706–85), Venetian composer. A 'toccata' is a fast, light piece of keyboard music which is often intended to exhibit the prowess of the player. **6 St Marks:** cathedral in Venice; **Doges ... rings:** a ceremony at which officials of Venice cast a ring into the sea to symbolise Venice's maritime power. **8 Shylock's bridge:** the Rialto bridge (*Merchant of Venice*, I.3.105). **18 clavichord:** stringed keyboard instrument. **19 lesser thirds:** beginning of a series of musical terms in the poem.

**p. 42 *Any Wife to Any Husband*:** First published in *Men and Women*. May have biographical origins; Browning's father was successfully sued for breach of promise in 1852; Browning's mother had died three years previously. **18 soul makes all things new:** see Revelations xxi.5. **77 Titian's Venus:** Titian's painting *Venus of Urbino*. **94 sealing up the sum:** see Ezekiel xxvii.12.

**p. 47 *Mesmerism*:** Published in *Men and Women*. **45 calotypist:** photographer. **75 tractile:** obedient; capable of being directed.

**p. 52 *'Childe Roland to the Dark Tower Came'*:** First published in *Men and Women*. A 'childe' is a young man who wishes to become a knight. The title is from Edgar in Shakespeare's *King Lear*, III.4.179. **137 like galley-slaves:** alluding to a Turkish entertainment in which galley-slaves were set against each other: **143 Tophet:** Biblical valley of fire, symbolising hell. **160 Apollyon:** the devil. See Revelations ix.11 and Bunyan's *Pilgrim's Progress*. **203 slug-horn:** battle trumpet.

**p. 59 *Bishop Blougram's Apology*:** Published in *Men and Women*. Blougram is a fictional character, as is Gigadibs the journalist. Browning's models for the Bishop may have included Cardinal Wiseman (1801–65) and Cardinal Newman (1801–90). **3 Abbey:** Westminster Abbey, taken over from the Catholic Church by Henry VIII. **6 Pugin:** A.W.N. Pugin (1812–52), architect and designer. A leader of the Gothic Revival, he was also a convert to Catholicism. **Corpus Christi Day:** the Thursday after Trinity Sunday, commemorating the Eucharist. **45 Che ch' è:** Italian exclamation, literally meaning 'what? what?', used to register disbelief or denial. **52 Goethe:** Johann Wolfgang von Goethe (1749–1832), German writer. **54 Count D'Orsay:** (1801–52), a famous dandy. **70 tire-room:** dressing-room. **109 Balzac:** Honoré de Balzac (1799–1850), French novelist. **112 Leipsic:** the Teubner series of classical texts, the first of which was published in 1849. **114 Jerome:** a painting of St Jerome by Correggio in Parma. **115 Correggio:** Antonio Allegri (c. 1489–1534), painter called Correggio after the town where he was born. Said to have studied at Modena (line 118). **185 Euripides:** (BC 480–06), Greek dramatist. **191 The grand Perhaps!:** echoes Rabelais's supposed death-bed utterance, 'I go to seek a grand perhaps.' **317 Peter's creed . . . Hildebrand's:** St Peter was the first Pope. Hildebrand (Pope Gregory VII from 1073) made claims for the worldly power of the Church. **382 Verdi:** Giuseppe Verdi (1813–1901), composer, mainly of operas (his *Macbeth* is referred to here; it was reportedly received in silence by fellow composer Rossini). **398 demireps:** women of ill-repute. **412 Schelling:** Frederick William Joseph von Schelling (1775–1854), German philosopher. **426 Peter's chains:** in Acts 12.7 Peter's chains are removed by an angel. **427 Noodledom:** the realm of stupidity. **467 'The state, that's I':** said by Louis XIV, not Napoleon. **473 Austrian marriage:** Napoleon married Marie Louise of Austria in 1810. **476 Austerlitz:** where Napoleon defeated the Russians and Austrians in 1805. **515 trimmest house:** New Place, Shakespeare's house from 1597. **517 Guilio Romano:** Italian painter (c. 1492–1546) referred to in *The Winter's Tale*; **Dowland:** John Dowland (1526–1626), lutanist and composer, mentioned in Shakespeare's *The Passionate Pilgrim*. **520 'Pandulph . . . cardinal':** from *King John*, III.i.138. **534 Terni:** town in Italy. **Gothard's top:** St Gothard's Pass in the Alps; **554:** 'cousin', Blougram assumes, is the form of address he would have used, as a Papal representative, for Elizabeth I (Queen Bess). **569 Luther:** Martin Luther (1483–1546), German religious reformer. **573 re-opens a shut book:** refers to Luther's translation of the Bible into vernacular. **578 Strauss:** David Friedrich Strauss (1808–74), biblical critic. **665 ichors:** liquids from wounds which help healing. **668 Michael's foot:** the archangel Michael is often depicted standing upon or astride a snake to symbolise the casting of Satan from Heaven. **686 Ararat:** the mountain where Noah's ark landed (Genesis 8.4). **716 King Bomba:** Ferdinand II (1810–59), King of the Two Sicilies; **lazzaroni:** beggars. **717 Antonelli:** Cardinal, secretary to Pius IX. **729 Naples' liquefaction:** the liquefaction of the patron saint of Naples, St Januarius; Newman defended belief in this event. **733 decrassify:** purify. **745 Fichte's clever cut:** Johann Gottlieb Fichte (1762–1814), German philosopher who believed that God was an idea invented by humanity. **792 Scouts:** mocks. **834 French book:** probably Diderot's *Supplément au Voyage be Bougainville*. **878 *'Pastor est tui Dominus'*:** 'The

Lord is your Shepherd'. **916 Albano:** site of Roman ruins; **Anacreon:** Greek lyric poet living in sixth century BC. **943 drugget:** coarse material; **purple:** colour of royalty. **946 Blackwood's magazine:** influential Victorian magazine. **948 Germans:** refers to predominance of Germans in nineteenth-century Shakespeare studies. **973–4 in partibus ... non:** 'Bishops in regions, and also . . .' A bishop *in partibus infidelium* has charge of a place beyond the influence of the Church. In 1850, because of the re-establishment of the Catholic hierarchy in England, Wiseman changed from being a bishop *in partibus* to being Bishop of Westminster. **998 cavillers:** quibblers. **999 Oppugn:** assail, oppose. **1014 last chapter of St John:** a confusing ending, referring either to 'knowledge of the gospels' or more specifically to the miracle of the fishes in John 21.

**p. 86 *Holy-Cross Day*:** First published in *Men and Women*. Holy-Cross Day is 14 September. It commemorates the Emperor Constantine's vision of a cross in the sky. **1 Fee, faw, fum!:** Recalls the Giant's words in the story of Jack the Giant-Killer. Perhaps appropriate here because in some versions the giant smells the blood of a Christian (as opposed to an English) man. **23 chine:** backbone. **52 Corso:** main street in Rome. **66 Ben Ezra's Song of Death:** Abraham Ben Meir Ezra (c. 1092–1167), Jewish scholar. His 'Song of Death' is an invention of Browning's. See Browning's poem 'Rabbi Ben Ezra' in *Dramatis Personae* (1864). **73–8:** see Isaiah xiv for the source of this prophecy. **85–90:** echoing Mark xiii.32–7. **104 Barabbas:** a significant figure in this context since he was the man whom the Jews asked Pilot to release in preference to Jesus (Mark xv.6–14). **111 Ghetto:** Jewish area of the town, derived from the Italian 'Borghetto' ('little town'). **120 Pleasant Land:** Jeremiah iii.18–19.

**p. 91 *Two in the Campagna*:** The Campagna is the countryside around Rome.

**p. 94 *Caliban Upon Setebos*:** First published in *Dramatis Personae* (1864). Caliban is the 'monster' from Shakespeare's *The Tempest*. Caliban's mother, Sycorax, is said in *The Tempest* to have worshipped Setebos. Caliban talks about himself in the third person throughout. The epigraph is from Psalms 50.21. **5 eft-things:** newts. **7 pompion-plant:** a type of pumpkin. **16 dam:** mother, i.e. Sycorax. **20 Prosper and Miranda:** Caliban's master and the master's daughter: **50 pie:** a pied bird. **71 bladdery:** bubbly. **79 hoopoe:** a colourful crested bird. **83 grigs:** grasshoppers or crickets. **148 hips:** fruit of the wild rose. **156 oncelot:** ocelot.

**157 ounce:** lynx. **161 Ariel:** in *The Tempest*, Prospero's fairy-like servant. **229 urchin:** hedgehog. **294 quails:** Numbers II.31–2.